Building Relationships

Developing Skills for Life

David H. Olson

John DeFrain

Amy K. Olson

Building Relationships
Developing Skills for Life

Published by **Life Innovations, Inc.**
P.O. Box 190
Minneapolis, MN 55440-0190

Copyright Information

Copyright © 1999
Life Innovations, Inc.

Library of Congress

Olson, David H., DeFrain, John & Olson, Amy.

Building Relationships: Developing Skills for Life/
Life Innovations.

Includes bibliographical references.
ISBN   0967198305   (paper)
1. Man-women relationships 2. Communication 3. Title

Purchase of Book

This book can be purchased on the website or by calling Life Innovations. Quantity discounts are available.

Life Innovations, Inc.
P.O. Box 190
Minneapolis, MN 55440-0190

Toll free number: (800) 331-1661
www.Lifeinnovations.com

Table of Contents

Preface

Goals for this Book:

The title of this book, **Building Relationships: Developing Skills for Life**, clearly describes the primary goals of this book. It is designed to help people learn about how to build relationships with others, including peers and family. The book describes healthy relationship attitudes and ideas so that individuals can develop and maintain close relationships with others. The relationship skills described in the book and practiced in the exercises include assertiveness, active listening and conflict resolution.

Topics for the Chapters:

The 13 topics selected for chapters include the most important relationship areas for those interested in dating, mate selection and marriage. These topics also are part of the **PREPARE Program** for couples planning to marry. The chapters include relationship skills like communication, conflict resolution and other areas that are often problematic for couples such as finances, family of origin, roles and values and beliefs.

Active Learning Using AWARE Quiz:

Each chapter begins with a *self-scoring AWARE Quiz* that a person is encouraged to take *before* reading the chapter and again *after* reading the chapter. Each AWARE Quiz focuses on important relationship attitudes and ideas. The answers to each Quiz are contained in the chapter and are the primary focus of each chapter.

Acknowledgements:

We first wish to thank all those who have encouraged us to write this book over the years, particularly Karen Olson. We also appreciated the editorial comments and suggestions provided by Nikki DeFrain and Sharlene Fye. We greatly appreciated the excellent job on the graphics and book design provided by Rob & Mina Will and revisions by Kevin & Mary Lou Hay of Will Graphics.

Dedicated to Karen Olson & Nikki DeFrain:

This book would not have been created without the inspiration of Karen Olson. She encouraged and supported her husband, David Olson, and daughter, Amy Olson, as they struggled with the many challenging steps required to complete this book. Her suggestions, guidance and numerous editorial reviews were invaluable.

Nikki DeFrain was a strong emotional support to John DeFrain and assisted in editing the early versions of this book with many useful ideas.

To Young People:

This book was designed specifically for you. It is designed to help you improve your relationships with others—your friends, your peers, your family and others that are important to you. The older you get, the more you value good relationships with others. Maintaining a good relationship with others requires good communication and relationship skills and this is a major focus of the book.

When you are dating, the better the relationship skills you have, the better chance you have of developing and maintaining a good relationship with that person. This book is designed to help you get along with those with whom you want to have a close and loving relationship.

To Parents:

Raising an adolescent or young adult is often very challenging. It is a stressful and difficult time for young adults because they are seeking their independence and parents are trying to maintain some control over the process. It is also a very difficult time to talk with each other about important issues.

This book is designed for you as parents to better connect and communicate on important topics and issues to discuss with your adolescent or young adult. We highly recommend that you read this book and then encourage your child to read it.

One idea is to create a family time (about 30 minutes) each week where you can discuss the items and issues related to a given chapter. Even though this will not always be easy to do, you will find that the experience will improve your long term family relationship.

To Teachers/Leaders using the book in Classes/Groups:

This book is designed to help you more effectively connect with adolescents and young people in groups. There is an AWARE Quiz at the beginning of each chapter which is designed as an outline for the chapter and the chapter provides the answers to the questions.

The ten-item AWARE Quiz in each chapter can be useful to you in a variety of ways. First it can be used as an outline for lecturing and discussing issues. It provides a list of significant issues that are important to discuss and debate in a group.

There is a Teacher's Manual that contains many suggestions and masters for transparencies from the book that you can use. A variety of exercises are designed to be used in class and out of class with peers and parents. The manual also contains an overall quiz that can be used to assess student progress by assessing the class response before and after the course.

Authors

David H. Olson, Ph.D., is Professor Emeritus, Family Social Science, University of Minnesota, St. Paul, MN and is President of Life Innovations. He is a developer of the PREPARE/ENRICH Program for Couples. He is past President, *National Council on Family Relations* and a Fellow and clinical member in the *American Psychological Association (APA)* and the *American Association of Marital and Family Therapy (AAMFT)*. He has written 20 books and over 100 articles in the field of marriage and family. His most recent books include *Marriage and Family: Diversity and Strengths* (2000) and *Empowering Couples: Building on Your Strengths* (2000).

John DeFrain, Ph.D., is Professor of Family Science at the University of Nebraska-Lincoln. He is past director of the Marital and Family Therapy Program. He has done extensive research on family strengths in over 20 countries. He has published over 15 books including: *Marriage and Family: Diversity and Strengths* (2000), and *Secrets of Strong Families* (1985).

Amy K. Olson, B.A., is Research Associate at Life Innovations, Minneapolis, MN. She co-authored an article entitled *Prepare/Enrich Program: Version 2000* and co-authored the book *Empowering Couples: Building on Your Strengths* (2000). She served as student representative on the Board of Directors of the *Minnesota Council of Family Relations (MCFR)*.

Marriage and Families Today

> ❝ Other things may change us, but we start and end with our family. ❞
>
> ANTHONY BRANDT

Aware Quiz

Marriage and Family Facts

Circle True or False

1 Most of the information we have about families from
television shows and movies is about real-life families.   T or F

2 An unmarried mother with a child is not a family.   T or F

3 The most common type of family is one in which both parents live
with their own children.   T or F

4 By their 18th birthday, more than half of today's children will
have lived in a single-parent household.   T or F

5 Most people who get divorced don't ever remarry.   T or F

6 People often think about the strengths they have in their families.   T or F

7 More than half (50%) of the couples getting married today
will get divorced.   T or F

8 The average length of a marriage that ends in divorce is seven years.   T or F

9 The older you are when you marry, the better the chances are
that you will have a happy marriage.   T or F

10 A marriage can be saved only if both partners are
committed to improving it.   T or F

*Please complete the QUIZ
before reading the chapter.*

2

What is a Family?

Almost everyone grows up in a family, and most people plan to create their own families someday. The term family evokes different images and ideas in each of us because we all have unique and very personal experiences of family. Most of our knowledge about families comes from our own experience growing up in a family. No two people share the exact same family experiences, even those who grow up in the same family.

How the Media Defines Family

Unfortunately, the mass media—television, radio, the movies, newspapers and magazines—strongly influence how we as individuals define family. We say "unfortunately" because the picture of family painted by the mass media usually bears little resemblance to how families really are. The families we see on film and read about in the pages of our daily newspapers are probably sexier, chattier, more violent, more problem-prone, richer or poorer, and in general lead much more dramatic lives than the average American family.

As consumers, we may be lulled into thinking we are seeing a very realistic "slice of life," but the slice we are served usually represents relatively extreme, out-of-the-ordinary family behaviors that grab the viewer's attention, ensuring advertisers a good chance of selling their products. So we often see unrealistic examples of families in the media and rarely see how more typical families live.

Most of us are in the difficult position of trying to understand families with very limited resources to help us. We may fall into the trap of generalizing about the way families really are based on our own experience growing up in our family or what we see in the media. In reality, families are diverse in how they look, how they are organized and how they deal with various members.

This can be particularly problematic for children who grow up in very troubled families. If much of what a person sees at home is violence and pain, they are likely to conclude at a young age that families are places where people hurt each other, and that hurting each other is normal. The mass media, with their relentless focus on life's conflicts and problems, may not give a much more realistic picture of what a genuinely healthy family environment looks like. If you don't know that healthy families exist, you don't know what to look for in life to be happy.

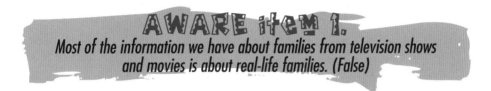

AWARE item 1.
Most of the information we have about families from television shows and movies is about real-life families. (False)

The Dictionary Definition

The mass media tends to give us negative or unrealistic impressions of what families are like. The dictionary is more straightforward. For example, the American Heritage Dictionary defines family as:

1. Parents and their children.
2. A group of persons related by blood or marriage.
3. The members of one household.
4. A group of things with common characteristics.

Try doing this: Make a list of the members of your family—as you define your family—and see if your family fits one of the dictionary definitions of family.

AWARE item 2.
An unmarried mother with a child is not a family. (False)

Your Definition of Family

If you were to write a definition of *family,* what would it be? There is clearly no one definition because there are so many different kinds of families. Family types are as varied as the individuals who live in families. There are the traditional two-parent families, there are one-parent families, families without children, and many variations of stepfamilies. All are different family forms. No one type of family is better than any other. A happy one-parent family, for example, can be a better place for a child to grow up than a troubled two-parent family.

One admittedly biased definition of family—but one that we especially like—is *"people who love and care for each other."* Not all families today fit that definition, of course, but what a wonderful world it would be if all family members could find ways to love and care for each other.

AWARE item 3.
The most common type of family is one in which both parents live with their own children. (False)

What do Families Do?

Although the characteristics and the structures of families differ greatly, the functions of families are usually quite similar. The family we grow up in is especially significant to us because it provides for so many of our needs, including basic and economic needs, emotional needs, and social needs.

Basic and **economic needs** include food, shelter, clothing, and health care. These are all the things we take for granted as children—if we are lucky enough to be born into a family that can provide all these needs.

Emotional needs include emotional support and acceptance, nurturing, and security. These are all provided, ideally, on an unconditional basis to all family members. In short, the family provides us with support because we're part of the family.

Social needs involve the family's role in the socialization of it's children. *Socialization* is the process by which children learn what behaviors are acceptable within the family and in other social environments. Children learn these socially acceptable behaviors by observation, imitation, and reinforcement from parents and other family members. Our family also is the link that connects us to other social institutions, such as churches and synagogues, schools, and friends.

As children get older, more of their needs are met by people and institutions outside their family. Initially, though, the main source of fulfillment is the family, and the family often continues to be a primary source well into adulthood.

Is the Family Changing?

The traditional American family—an employed father, a homemaker mother, and two children—is not so common anymore. In fact, this family structure accounts for less than a quarter of today's families. In the 1950's more than 70 percent of families consisted of a working father and a mother who stayed home. Today, only 33 percent of all the families in this country are made up of working husbands and stay-at-home wives; about 15 percent of these are families with children.

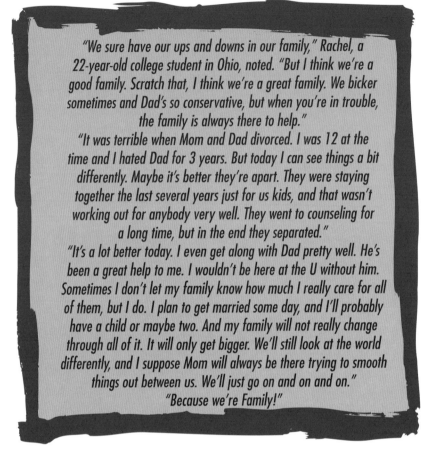

"We sure have our ups and downs in our family," Rachel, a 22-year-old college student in Ohio, noted. "But I think we're a good family. Scratch that, I think we're a great family. We bicker sometimes and Dad's so conservative, but when you're in trouble, the family is always there to help."

"It was terrible when Mom and Dad divorced. I was 12 at the time and I hated Dad for 3 years. But today I can see things a bit differently. Maybe it's better they're apart. They were staying together the last several years just for us kids, and that wasn't working out for anybody very well. They went to counseling for a long time, but in the end they separated."

"It's a lot better today. I even get along with Dad pretty well. He's been a great help to me. I wouldn't be here at the U without him. Sometimes I don't let my family know how much I really care for all of them, but I do. I plan to get married some day, and I'll probably have a child or maybe two. And my family will not really change through all of it. It will only get bigger. We'll still look at the world differently, and I suppose Mom will always be there trying to smooth things out between us. We'll just go on and on and on."

"Because we're Family!"

Trends in Family Structure

Single-parent families are increasing. According to the U.S. Bureau of the Census (1998) in the 1970s, only 12 percent of the children in the United States lived in a single-parent home. In 1980 the number had increased to 22 percent; by 1990 the figure was 28 percent; and by 1997, 30 percent. Social scientists predict that 60 percent of children who are 2 years old today will have lived in a single-parent household by the time they are 18 years of age.

AWARE item 4.

By their 18th birthday, more than half of today's children will have lived in a single-parent household. (True)

The number of **stepfamilies**—families in which one or both of the partners have children from a previous marriage—is also growing. In 1997, 20 percent of the families in the United States were stepfamilies, also called blended families. Rising divorce and remarriage rates are the main reasons for the increase in the numbers of stepfamilies. About 75 percent of people who divorce eventually marry again.

Figure 1-1.
Family Structure in the United States

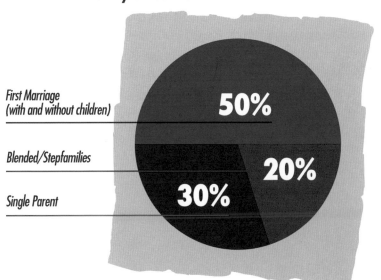

First Marriage
(with and without children)

Blended/Stepfamilies

Single Parent

50%

20%

30%

AWARE item 5.
Most people who get divorced don't ever remarry. (False)

Families today are having considerably fewer children, except for certain ethnic groups. In 1970 more than half of 40-year-old women had three or more children; by 1994 the percentage had dropped to less than 30 percent. Currently, the average number of children per family in the United States is 1.7.

In many two parent families, both partners work outside the home. In nearly 60 percent of United States families, both parents work full-time. In many others (16 percent), the father works full-time and the mother works part-time.

Characteristics of Strong Families

All families have problems, and all families have strengths. We often focus too much attention on our problems, and not enough on our strengths. In fact, most people are not aware of the strengths their family has. *Think about what strengths there are in your family.*

AWARE item 6.
People often think about the strengths they have in their families. (False)

Qualities of Strong Families

There is no "right" way to be a family. The perfect family does not exist. But our research on strong families indicates that six qualities are common in happy, emotionally healthy families:

1. Commitment to the family.
2. Appreciation and affection for one another.
3. Positive communication.
4. Spending enjoyable time together in adequate amounts.
5. A sense of spiritual well-being.
6. The ability to cope with stress and crisis.

Box 1-1 Summarizes Qualities of Strong Families.

Box 1-1.

Qualities of Strong Families

Commitment
Trust
Honesty
Dependability
Faithfulness

Appreciation and Affection
Caring for each other
Friendship
Respect for individuality
Playfulness & Humor

Positive Communication
Sharing feelings
Giving compliments
Avoiding blame
Being able to compromise
Agreeing to disagree

Time Together
Quality time in great quantity
Good things take time
Enjoying each other's company
Simple good times
Sharing fun times

Spiritual Well-Being
Faith
Compassion
Shared ethical values
Oneness with humankind

Ability to Cope with Stress
Adaptability
Growing through crises together
Openness to change
Resilience

The State of Marriage Today

Marriage is still very popular in the United States with over 90 % of people getting married at least once. But, unfortunately, over 50 % of couples getting married today get divorced, many after only 3 years of marriage.

There are many positive reasons to marry. Married couples, compared to singles, tend to be happier, more emotionally stable, more physically healthy, more wealthy, have a better sexual relationship and live longer.

The fact that over 50 % of couples getting married today eventually get divorced says that couples are not prepared for the challenges of marriage. Part of the reason for the high divorce rate is that couples spend too much time preparing for the wedding, which lasts a day, and they spend little time preparing to be a good partner, which is intended to last a lifetime. Good marriage preparation programs, which will be described in Chapter 4, can greatly improve the chances for a successful marriage.

AWARE item 7.
More than half (50 percent) of the couples getting married today will get divorced. (True)

Why Do So Many Marriages End in Divorce?

Unfortunately, the average length of a marriage that ends in divorce in the United States is only seven years. Marriage is very risky and it is hard to achieve and maintain a happy marriage.

Love is not enough for creating a happy marriage. Couples often think that just being in love is sufficient reason to get married and that love alone will make them happily married forever. But to make a happy marriage you need to have good communication skills and know how to discuss and resolve differences.

Individuals in unhappy marriages often blame the problems they have on each other. In fact, many people lack the relationship skills to deal successfully with the challenges that marriage offers. Building and maintaining a happy marriage relationship takes a thoughtful attitude, teamwork, creativity, and considerable effort.

AWARE item 8.
The average length of a marriage that ends in divorce is seven years. (True)

There are many reasons for the high divorce rate and the fact that many marriages don't last very long. A classic study by Stan Albrecht of 500 divorced people who remarried asked individuals to rank-order the reasons for the failure of their marriages. These are the top ten reasons they listed: infidelity (sex outside of marriage), no longer loving each other, emotional problems, financial problems, physical abuse, alcohol, sexual problems, problems with in-laws, neglect of children, and communication problems.

Age and maturity are also important factors. The ages of the couple at the time of marriage is predictive of the likelihood of divorce, especially if the couple are still teenagers. In fact, 85 percent of couples who marry before age 20 will eventually divorce. Younger couples are less likely to be emotionally mature. People grow and change a lot in their late teens and early twenties, and they often grow apart instead of together. Also, younger people are at a disadvantage in the working world. They lack the education and experience necessary to acquire a good job, which contributes to the stability of a marriage. Most experts agree that the older you are when you marry, the more likely you are to have a happy marriage.

AWARE item 9.
The older you are when you marry, the better the chances are that you will have a happy marriage. (True)

Many Marriages Fail Because of Lack of Commitment

Many people go into marriage with unrealistic expectations. People often believe that they will marry and then live "happily ever after" as people do in fairy tales. "Happily ever after" is possible, but it takes commitment and effort to make it happen.

A common reason that couples divorce is because of a lack of commitment and relationship skills to develop a happy marriage. Individuals commonly say that they are "no longer in love." In many of these cases, one or both partners have hidden their unhappiness and avoided discussing it. Eventually all the feelings they had toward each other—both positive and negative—disappear. In some cases the couple lose interest in each other, and in other cases the couple focus so completely on their problems that they lose sight of their strengths. If both partners are willing to repair their marriage, they can work on building the strengths they still have as a couple and on developing new strengths. But a marriage cannot be saved unless both partners commit to the effort.

AWARE item 10.
A marriage can be saved only if both partners are committed to improving it. (True)

Prevention is much easier than cure. Just as it is much easier to maintain your car than it is to fix it once it has broken down, it is easier to maintain your relationship over time, than to put it back together once it falls apart. Couples who wait too long to make "repairs" often don't have the desire to fix their relationship. Ignoring feelings about each other and their relationship is likely to lead to lack of interest in one another.

Trends in Marriage

Marriage continues to be one of the most popular institutions, with more than 90 percent of all American adults marrying at least once. Although this figure has not changed significantly since the 1960s, the following trends have occurred:

- More individuals are delaying marriage until their late twenties. The age at which people get married has increased the last 30 years. Currently, the average age for first marriage is 26.7 years for men and 24.5 years for women. **This is the oldest average age for marriage for both men and women in American history.** In 1960, the average age for first marriage was 22.8 years for men and 20.3 years for women.

- More couples are living together (cohabiting) before marriage, and cohabitation is becoming more tolerated in our society. The rate of cohabitation has increased at least sixfold since the 1960s, with about 2.5 million unmarried couples living together in 1988, and over 5 million cohabitating in 2000. Most cohabitating adults have never been married.

Families are Changing

The family is perhaps society's oldest and most resilient institution. From the beginning of human life, people have grouped themselves into families to find emotional, physical, and communal support. Although in recent years, people have predicted the demise of the family, it not only survives but continues to change and evolve. Family structures may vary in this country and around the world, but the value of "family" endures.

Families can provide intimacy and closeness, but they can also create disagreement and conflict. In this book we focus on how individuals can work together to develop and maintain satisfying personal relationships, both within the family and outside the family. The goal of healthy and happy relationships is well worth the effort.

Now that you've finished reading Chapter 1, why not go back and take the AWARE Quiz, "Marriage and Family Facts," again and see if you've learned something new.

Dating and Mate Selection

> ❝ We wish you
> two gifts of life:
> love of learning and
> learning to love. ❞
>
> Dr. D.H. Olson

Aware Quiz

Dating & Mating

Circle True or False

1 Being in love is an important aspect of an arranged marriage.   T or F

2 Dating a variety of people helps you get to know yourself and others.   T or F

3 If you feel attracted to someone, it means you would make a great couple.   T or F

4 Choosing a date should be like choosing a friend.   T or F

5 Who you marry significantly affects the course of your life.   T or F

6 The criteria for evaluating a date should be the same as for selecting a mate.   T or F

7 The way a couple relates during dating will carry over into marriage.   T or F

8 It is easy to change habits and behaviors that you dislike in your partner.   T or F

9 A good way to predict a partner's behavior in marriage is to observe how the person relates to his/her parents and family.   T or F

10 The more differences you have as a dating couple, the more often there will be conflict and problems in marriage.   T or F

Please complete the QUIZ before reading the chapter.

Dating: An American Invention

America created the current dating system, which is becoming the primary way couples select each other for marriage around the world. But historically, a variety of matchmaking approaches have been used in different countries.

All societies have created some kind of system for matching individuals for marriage and parenthood. These systems range from a village religious leader selecting a mate according to astrological signs to individual choice based on personal attraction and love. In some cultures, couples are matched while they are still infants. In others, the bride or groom must prove fertility by producing children before either is eligible for marriage. Although the customs of mate selection vary widely, all perform a necessary function of matching a couple for marriage and, in most cases, eventual parenthood.

Historical Perspectives on Dating

Throughout most of world history, courtship was generally brief. In most cultures, the parents of the bride and groom selected the future spouse and made most of the arrangements for the marriage ceremony. If the prospective couple were granted any freedom of choice, they were expected to complete their arrangements in a few days. The pattern common in our culture, in which individuals spend months or even years in dating and choosing a mate, developed largely within the past century.

Parent-arranged marriage is based on the principle that the elders in a community have the wisdom to select the appropriate spouse. Up to three-quarters of marriages in some cultures may still be "arranged." Parents or elders are likely to base their decisions on economic, political, and social status. Arranged marriages serve to extend existing family units rather than to create new units, for the newlyweds are likely to live with one set of their parents. In these cultures, lineage and family status are generally more important than love or affection. Increasingly, the parents in these cultures are giving the couple's preferences some consideration.

Although young adults in the United States might view the practice of parent-arranged marriage as strange and uncivilized, many young people and older people prefer it. Some observers have noted that most participants in such systems tend to view the process favorably.

In India, for example, it has been reported that some young people become distressed if they have to choose their own mate, fearing they might make the wrong choice.

The world appears to be moving toward freedom of choice in marriage. This approach is sometimes called a *"love match"*. The movement away from arranged marriage appears to be related to industrialization. As countries change from more rural to urban/industrial societies, love marriages become more common. Researchers have found that the ability of women to work outside the home leads to the decline of arranged marriages, enhances the possibility of love matches, and may slightly reduce the marriage rate.

In the past, parents typically exercised considerable influence over courtship and the choice of a mate. Young people were usually tied to the home and, except for the occasional community social event, had little opportunity to escape the watchful eyes of their parents. Opportunities for dating were infrequent. Courtship was a rather formal event, often conducted under parental supervision. Males were expected to get the permission of the female's parents and to initiate the acquaintance. Although the couples were generally allowed the privilege of making up their own minds, family members usually announced their approval (or disapproval) before the relationship got too serious. But young people were granted much more freedom of individual choice than exists in parent-arranged courtship systems.

As America became more industrialized and parents began to work away from the home, young people gained considerable freedom from parental supervision, as well as responsibility for organizing their free time. *Dating,* or individual-choice courtship, emerged as an activity in its own right, creating a new institution within the culture. This pattern, with some variation, appears to be common as societies change from rural to industrial.

Along with the emergence of individual-choice courtship and a defined period for dating, permissiveness in behavior also increased. The term *permissiveness* refers to the extent to which couples are physically intimate before marriage. Historically, males were permitted greater freedom and privilege than females in dating. However, the same basic forces that produced the revolution in dating customs in industrial societies also fostered a decline in the *double standard*—different standards of dating and social behavior for men than for women. As customs changed, women became more assertive in dating. Although many females still expect males to call them, to plan dates, and to propose marriage, females today generally are more assertive and participate more actively in the dating process than they did in earlier generations.

Today people are dating sooner and also in a more casual fashion than earlier generations. Dating now commonly begins in preadolescence as a group experience where individuals attend get-togethers. Steady dating is still popular, but adolescents have relaxed many of the requirements of exclusivity and commitment that were the norm in the past.

There is also evidence that young people are forming more cross-sex friendships than in earlier generations and are placing more emphasis on developing close friendships. Adolescents today are forming more of a network of friends during the courtship period than earlier generations did. Courtship customs are less oriented toward marriage than in earlier periods. Young people are less eager to become formally engaged and are delaying marriage. The divorce statistics appear to be influencing this thinking, causing young people to approach marriage with more reservations.

Arranged Marriage vs. Love-Match Marriage

In arranging a marriage for their children, parents in a traditional society do not focus on love, but on more external considerations: economic security, a stable family and choosing a mate who will be a good parent. Although love between husband and wife may develop as time goes by, there are clearly more important things to consider. Divorce rates in societies in which arranged marriages are common tend to be much lower than divorce rates in societies in which love matches are common. This gives some credibility to the argument that parents are better able to make good decisions about prospective partners than are young people themselves.

AWARE item 1.
Being in love is an important aspect of an arranged marriage. (False)

Table 2-1 clearly summarizes the differences between love matches and arranged marriages.

Table 2-1.

Comparison of Love Matches (Couple's Choice) and Arranged Marriages (Parents' Choice)		
Aspect	**Love Match**	**Arranged Marriage**
Dating	Top priority	Not encouraged
Love	Very necessary	Not necessary
Personal knowledge of partner	Considerable knowledge	Little to some knowledge
Shared values	Somewhat important	Very important
Time together	Lots	Little
Sexual relationship	Some	Usually none
Parental approval	Somewhat important	Critical

In the United States today, we clearly are a culture of love-match marriages rather than arranged marriages, but many parents still wield a good deal of influence on their child's choice of a mate. If a young person's parents disapprove of their child's choice of a partner, the young person might not necessarily decide to drop the partner, but would clearly have a difficult time dealing with the parents' concern. Some parents may feel that a "wrong" choice is a partner from a different religion, ethnic group, social class or education level. Even though we lean toward love matches in our country, many parents exercise subtle and sometimes not-so-subtle pressure in favor of some prospective partners and against others.

In cultures in which arranged marriages are common, children can exercise subtle and not-so-subtle influences on their parents' choice of a partner. One young Indian man in Fiji told us, for example, that his parents arranged his marriage for him:

> *But, I knew this beautiful girl from school, and I really liked her. So, I told my brother to suggest her to my parents as a good marriage possibility for me. He wasn't supposed to tell them that's what I wanted—just to very carefully point out all the good points about her and her family. And that's how it worked out. My brother gave them all the propaganda, and then my parents talked with her parents and they got it all worked out for us.*
>
> *"I call this a semiarranged marriage," the young man chuckled.*

Dating: Advantages and Limitations

One of the chief reasons so many marriages fail is that the functions of a date and a mate differ radically—that of a date is to be charming; that of a mate is to be responsible; and, unfortunately, the most charming individuals are not necessarily the most responsible, while the most responsible are just as often deficient in charm.

--SYDNEY HARRIS, JOURNALIST

Although dating customs have varied widely and have changed over the years, the basic functions of dating and courtship have remained consistent. Today the idea of dating in American culture is very important. Dating serves a number of useful purposes, but the dating system in this country is clearly not perfect. The advantages of dating are offset by several significant limitations.

Advantages of Dating

There are four distinct advantages of dating:

1. *Learning about differences in people.* Going out with different people helps us learn about the wide variety of individuals in our society. We are all, indeed, unique. Though we share important similarities, we also have our differences. Dating a variety of individuals helps us see these differences close up.

2. *Getting to know ourselves better.* Interacting with other people helps us see more clearly who we are. People think and act in a multitude of ways. Becoming more aware of these differences helps us to know ourselves better. We learn more about ourselves as we experience others who are very different from us in background, family, and personality.

3. *Learning about our likes and dislikes.* Dating helps us clarify what we are looking for in a partner, what we are comfortable with, and what makes us uncomfortable.

4. *Learning relationship skills.* Dating gives us lots of opportunities to practice relating to other people. We have to make all kinds of important decisions about what to say and do in the dating world, as well as consider how our behavior affects other people and how it affects us.

AWARE item 2.
Dating a variety of people helps you get to know yourself and others. (True)

Limitations of Dating

Clearly, dating can be a valuable series of experiences, helping us to gain knowledge of ourselves and others. But dating has several major shortcomings:

1. *Too much focus on showing only our positive self.* In general, when we date, we try very hard to show only our positive aspects. We tend to go to great lengths to hide any negative things that might offend the other person or cause our date to break off the relationship. There is nothing wrong with putting your best foot forward, but this tends to give individuals a skewed picture of each other. When the "real" person emerges after marriage, the partner can be surprised about how different this person really behaves.

2. *Isolation from other friends, family, and activities.* When we are involved in a serious dating relationship, it is very common to focus only on the dating partner, often neglecting other friends and family members. We may also pay less attention to school, work, and community activities that previously might have been very important to us.

3. *Failure to deal with common issues or problems.* In general, when we are seriously dating, we often avoid talking about differences we have or trying to settle relationship problems. We may gloss over them in an effort to maintain the positive excitement and fascination of the relationship. But problems that are not dealt with rarely go away; they simply smolder and turn into flames later.

4. *Poor preparation for marriage.* Though the dating system has many positive aspects, most professional observers (counselors, clergy, and psychologists) have been forced to conclude that dating alone is inadequate preparation for marriage. Couples need much more than the collection of experiences we call dating. They need a structured set of educational experiences about marriage: genuine preparation for one of life's most rewarding and difficult task, that of creating and maintaining a good marriage.

Physical Attraction

Physical attraction to another person is usually the first step in getting involved with that person. However, what a person is deep inside is much more important than the physical package we initially see. We know people whose beauty is only skin deep. We also know people who may not be all that attractive physically but who have a personality worth its weight in gold. Physical attraction plays a large part in starting a dating relationship but it can also lead couples away from what is more important in a relationship.

What Is Physical Attraction?

Physical attraction is the interest and excitement generated by various physical qualities of a person. "Beauty is in the eye of the beholder," the old saying goes. It means that different people find different physical qualities attractive, giving us all lots of opportunity to be attractive to others.

The list of physical qualities that are considered attractive from culture to culture is a long one and includes, in no particular order: facial features (eyes, smile, lips, nose, ears), hair, buttocks, waistline, overall physical attractiveness, weight, legs, breasts, skin, and figure. The items in each culture's list differ, and the order of importance also differs from culture to culture.

Furthermore, each individual's list is unique. Some people love broccoli; others hate it. Likewise, hair color or height might be crucial on one person's physical-attractiveness scale; another person might consider them totally irrelevant.

Perhaps most important of all, being physically attracted to an individual tells you very little about the person. A person may be physically attractive, but the more important qualities cannot be seen and must be discovered.

Physical Attractiveness and Dating

In the process of dating, physical attractiveness initially plays an important role. For example, researchers have found that physical attractiveness is one of the most important traits related to the frequency of being asked out on a first date. Physically attractive people are asked out more often. Fortunately, physical appearance is not everything. Those who don't look like movie stars can be attractive in other ways. For example, some have great personalities or special skills that others find interesting.

In the long run, physical attractiveness is not important in developing or sustaining a good relationship. It may get you a date, but it will not get you a long-term, happy relationship that can lead to a happy marriage.

Importance of Attractiveness to Males and Females

It is probably true that men are more interested in physical attractiveness in a date and women are more interested in personal qualities. The men in a study by Nevid (1984) described ten purely physical qualities; the women blended physical and personal qualities in their top-ten list. But when men and women rate the characteristics that are important for a *long-term relationship,* their lists are remarkably similar: honesty, personality, fidelity, sensitivity, warmth, kindness, character, tenderness, patience, and gentleness.

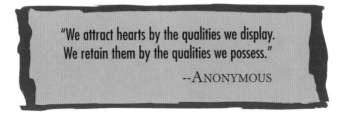

"We attract hearts by the qualities we display.
We retain them by the qualities we possess."

--ANONYMOUS

Physical Attraction and Compatibility

It is most important to remember that being physically attracted to someone does not predict compatibility. Liking the color of someone's hair or their figure or their smile tells us nothing about our chances for long-term success in a genuine relationship with that person. Compatibility has to be worked out over time. It takes good communication and conflict resolution skills to make a relationship successful (see more details in chapter 7 and 8).

AWARE item 3.
If you feel attracted to someone, it means you would make a great couple. (False)

Choosing a Dating Partner

Why are we attracted to some people and not to others? What keeps us together and happy as a couple for a long time? These are very important questions that have sparked countless serious research studies over the years.

Do Opposites Attract?

Talk with your friends about their boyfriends or girlfriends. "Are you alike?" you might ask. "Oh, no!" they will often reply. "He's so different from me. I'm talkative and outgoing, and he's shy. I'm interested in people, and he likes to read and stay at home working on projects."

This is an illustration of the notion that opposites attract. More formally called *complementary needs theory,* it states that people are attracted to someone whose personality complements (balances) their own personality. It assumes that we tend to seek out someone who has what we don't have but would like to have.

Many people are drawn to this idea because it seems to make a lot of sense on an intuitive level. But in most successful marriages, people are usually similar in many ways.

Do Birds of a Feather Flock Together?

Generally, couples who are attracted to one another and who stay together for a long time are rather similar. They tend to come from similar ethnic or cultural groups and social classes and hold similar religious perspectives and value systems. Couples tend to be about the same age and have a similar level of formal education. Their interests in life are similar, while they don't necessarily do everything together, they share important mutual interests. Couples have a solid foundation on which to build a lasting relationship.

This is not to say that Catholics cannot successfully marry Protestants or that European-Americans cannot marry African-Americans and live happily ever after. There are countless examples of couples who have crossed cultural and ethnic dividing lines and created strong relationships.

But, in general, people who get along well tend to have a lot in common. The most important things in life are things they share. This stands to reason because it's easier to relate to someone who looks at the world in the same way you do. For this reason, professionals commonly agree that if you want to create a long-term, stable relationship, you should look for a person with the qualities you would seek in a best friend.

Dating has many purposes: simple pleasure is one. Dating should be fun. But dating also has a very serious purpose: the search for a prospective mate. Confusion about why we are dating and what we are looking for long term can lead to disaster. If we are dating only for fun and pleasure, then a date with the qualities we value for pleasure would be adequate.

But because dating also has a more serious purpose for most people, we need to think long term. Beautiful eyes, long, wavy hair, and a nice body may be on the list of physical attributes that draw us to another person, but successful relationships are more than skin deep. Thinking in terms of friendship will help us find a person with lasting qualities. In the long run, we need to find someone who is physically attractive to us and, more important, whom we find to be emotionally compatible.

AWARE item 4.
Choosing a date should be like choosing a friend. (True)

Mate Selection

We tend to choose partners who are similar to us in a variety of ways—in ethnic and cultural background, age, educational and religious background, and socioeconomic status. Physical attractiveness also plays a large role in mate selection. What are the long-term effects of this decision?

The Importance of Partner Selection

Selecting a marriage partner may be the most important decision you make in life. Who you marry may significantly affect the course of your life in terms of where you live, whether you will have children and what they will be like, your occupation, your financial situation, and your general happiness. Let's say that one more time in a somewhat different way: who you marry will affect almost every aspect of your life, for better or worse. This is a decision that you cannot afford to take lightly.

AWARE item 5.
Who you marry significantly affects the course of your life. (True)

Dating versus Selecting a Mate

Dating a variety of people is necessary to decide what qualities we want in a date and eventually in a mate. But the focus of dating—at least in the early stages—should be on fun and on the opportunity it offers for self-discovery. It is important for dating couples not to rush into evaluating each date as a potential marriage.

We can make a mistake by going to extremes in either direction in the dating process. On the one hand, if we treat the process too seriously, we take all the fun out of it. We can scare away our dating partner before a good relationship has a chance to develop. In short, good things take time. A healthy relationship cannot be rushed.

On the other hand, if we are too easygoing about the process of dating, we may fail to see the serious, long-term consequences of a relationship with a person. Dating is a wonderful opportunity to learn about other people and about ourselves. As a dating relationship develops over time, we learn more and more about the person we are seeing and become more able to make a reasonable decision about their potential as a mate.

Some people believe that "you shouldn't date anyone you wouldn't marry." We think that is a bit too idealistic. You can date different people to find out what you enjoy in a dating partner and to think about what you might find pleasing in a lifelong mate. You simply cannot discover your preferences without interacting with many kinds of people in different dating situations.

We tend to be attracted to people because of physical attributes at first, and so someone who looks like a good date may turn out to be a poor prospect as a mate. A good date is someone you feel comfortable, safe, and happy with for a short period of time. But going out on a date is a kind of fairy-tale situation: you are both on your best behavior and you get to go home before you get on each other's nerves. Only time and a broad range of experiences together will tell you if a person might turn out to be a good mate.

One woman explained it this way:

> "He was so exciting when we were dating. I grew up in a farm family, and I was bored and looking for excitement. And, oh, we had so much fun together. But after we were married, I quickly discovered that excitement gets tiresome pretty quickly. On dates he was always so much fun. He was the life of the party. The fun ended soon after the wedding, though, because we never had any money".

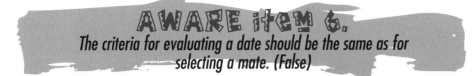

AWARE item 6.
The criteria for evaluating a date should be the same as for selecting a mate. (False)

What You See Is What You Get

We are generally on our best behavior during the early phases of dating. As the weeks and months go by, however, we become more "real" to one another. If two people relate well to one another and in a positive fashion during the later dating phases, they are more likely to do well after marriage. Similarly, if the dating relationship begins to go poorly, the problems are likely to continue after marriage. People often hope that things will get better after they are married. Instead, behavior we see while dating is very likely to continue after marriage and, in some cases, it gets worse.

AWARE item 7.
The way a couple relates during dating will carry over into marriage (True)

One of the most common myths some of us believe is that we can, through love and concern and hard work, change another person. Women, especially, seem susceptible to this belief:

> "I thought that because he cared about me he would change. I thought that if I invested all my time and love and energy in him, he would not be so selfish—that he would spend more time with me and less with his friends. I thought that after we got married he would realize how important the commitment he had made to me was. How wrong I was..."

AWARE item 8.
It is easy to change habits and behaviors that you dislike in your partner. (False)

Importance of Family-of-Origin

One of the best ways to learn about people is to observe them interacting with their parents and other family members—their *family-of-origin.* The kind of behavior we see in someone's family-of-origin gives us a great deal of information for predicting and understanding how he or she will relate to us after marriage. If an individual's family-of-origin communicates in an open and honest manner, that person is likely to relate in that same manner to us after marriage. If, on the other hand, an individual's family-of-origin is full of conflict, the individual is likely to carry that pattern into a couple relationship.

Many people believe that they will do everything in their power not to re-create their family-of-origin in a new family relationship. "I will not be like my father!" or "I'm not going to have a messed-up family like the one I grew up in!" they might say. This is much easier said than done. If our family members tend to be cranky, then that is the kind of behavior we are likely to continue in marriage. "The apple clearly does not fall far from the tree." This means that attitudes and behaviors usually do not differ greatly from the family tree from which they came. But you do have the power to recognize and change what you learned in your family.

AWARE item 9.
A good way to predict a partner's behavior in marriage is to observe how the person relates to his/her parents and family. (True)

The Filter Theory

One useful theory describing how people choose a mate is the **Filter Theory.** This theory suggests that people go through a complex filtering process that gradually narrows down the pool of possible dates to find a possible mate.

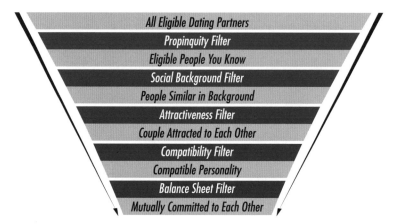

As you can see in the above figure the pool (number) of prospective partners gets smaller as individuals are eliminated (filtered out) because of differences of one sort or another. The influence of *propinquity,* or nearness in time and space, is the first filter. In other words, the pool of available partners consists of those living near us geographically or those with whom we are likely to come in contact.

Years ago, the marriage partner pool was limited by the difficulty of traveling long distances. More than half of those who married wed someone who lived within only a few miles of them. Although we now travel more extensively and have a broader range of social contacts, the pool of eligible partners is still influenced by our social circles, the school or church or synagogue we attend, the job we hold, and the types of activities in which we choose to participate.

Another factor that is changing the pool of possible dating partners for many people is the Internet. The potential pool is now less restricted to those physically nearby. A growing number of people are chatting online through subscription services or directly on the Internet and connecting with others of similar interests from across the country and even around the world. This trend will increase as online commercial dating services and other Internet services help us meet a broader cross-section of potential partners.

The *social background* filter determines the ethnic group, socio-economic stages, and age of potential partners. Individuals who believe marriage outside their own socioeconomic group is unacceptable eliminate outsiders from their pool of eligibles. As discussed earlier, the *physical attractiveness* is important in our selection of a date and potential mate. We tend to date individuals whom we consider as attractive or more so than we are.

Next, *compatibility* in personality, interests, and values acts as another filter in the mate selection process. At this more advanced stage, the pool of eligible partners has grown smaller, increasing the possibility of finding an acceptable partner. Finally we use the *balance sheet* filter; we evaluate what we are giving and what we are getting in the relationship. If our assessment is that the give-and-take is balanced, we often move on to a mutually committed relationship.

Conclusion

We've looked at how people chose a date and a mate. By analyzing the process, we may have taken some of the romance out of it. People enjoy "falling in love" and being "carried away with passion," but it's also important to learn to think about relationships while dating. We need to make good decisions about the person with whom we will spend our life. Marriage is too important to be left to chance or to be entered into without careful thought. A good marriage is a precious gift. A bad marriage can be a tragedy.

AWARE item 10.

The more differences you have as a dating couple, the more often there will be conflict and problems in marriage. (True)

Now that you have completed this chapter, you should go back to the AWARE Quiz on "Dating & Mating" and take it again. Then you can see how much you have learned!

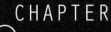

CHAPTER

3 **Love &**

Marriage

> " **Love cures people, both the ones who give it and the ones who receive it.** "
>
> DR. KARL MENNINGER

Aware Quiz

Love & Marriage

Circle True or False

1 The single best predictor of a successful marriage is the age of the couple. ⬤ T or F

2 The best relationships are those in which couples spend all their free time together. T or F

3 Getting married is a good way to establish independence from your family. T or F

4 Living together before marriage (cohabiting) helps couples develop a more satisfying marriage. T or F

5 Love is all you need for a happy marriage. T or F

6 Love is a good predictor of whether a marriage will last. T or F

7 The likelihood of divorce can be predicted from the quality of the relationship before marriage. T or F

8 Communication is the most useful and important skill couples can develop. T or F

9 Resolving differences before marriage makes marital happiness more likely. T or F

10 Differences in values can cause problems for couples. T or F

Please complete the QUIZ before reading the chapter.

Formula for a Successful Marriage

Marriage can be the most satisfying or the most frustrating experience of your life. In fact, many marriages are very satisfying in some ways and very frustrating in others. The following factors increase the chances for marital success. They are important things to keep in mind if you are thinking about marriage:

- *Both individuals should be independent and mature before marriage.* The more mature and independent two people are, the easier it is for them to develop an interdependent relationship that promotes intimacy. Independence and maturity often increase with age, a good reason for waiting to marry.

In fact, the single best predictor of a successful marriage is the age of the couple. The younger two people are at the time of their marriage, the greater their chance of divorce. This is partly because older people are typically more stable and know what they want in marriage.

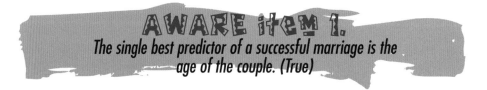

AWARE item 1.
The single best predictor of a successful marriage is the age of the couple. (True)

- *Both individuals love themselves as well as each other.* Self-esteem is very important in an intimate relationship. It is difficult to truly love another person if you don't love yourself. You need to feel secure and self-confident before you can be truly giving and loving to another.

- *Both individuals enjoy being alone as well as together.* To balance the separateness and togetherness that an intimate relationship requires, partners need to enjoy separate activities and time apart. Too much togetherness can lead to such negative behaviors as trying to control the partner and failing to appreciate the partner.

AWARE item 2.
The best relationships are those in which couples spend all their free time together. (False)

- *Both individuals are established in their job or career.* A stable and satisfying job or career fosters both financial and emotional security. When your job is going well, you can devote more time and energy to your relationship. On the other hand, the greater the stress at work, the less positive energy you have for a relationship. If you are planning a career, it is often better to start your career before you get married because you will be more able to focus on marriage.

- *Both individuals know themselves.* An intimate relationship requires openness and honesty between the partners. Each person must be able to evaluate their personal strengths and failings objectively and not blame their problems on other people. They must also know what they want from another person and also what they can give to a partner. Dating can help you learn about yourself and others.

- *Both individuals can express themselves assertively.* One key to developing intimacy is assertiveness—expressing what you want in a direct and generally positive manner. People who are not assertive in their communication often adopt a passive-aggressive approach, playing games and attempting to manipulate others. The more clearly partners ask for what they want from each other, the better the chances that the partner will comply. Don't confuse assertiveness with aggressiveness, which is an attempt to dominate another human being. Assertiveness is simply expressing one's own needs clearly and openly.

- *Both individuals try to satisfy each other's needs and tend not to be selfish.* When we focus on another's needs, we find that they tend to focus on our needs. This has been called the law of enlightened self-interest. The principle holds that being less selfish is in a person's best interest because it helps to build cooperative and intimate relationships that benefit everyone. Nonpossessive caring encourages the partner to grow and to reach her or his potential. Both partners generally benefit.

Gloria Steinem, an American writer, gets to the heart of the matter: "There are many more people trying to meet the right person than trying to become the right person." For some facts about marriage today, see Box 3-1.

BOx 3-1.

Facts about Marriage

• Approximately 2.4 million couples marry each year.

• Approximately 1.2 million couples divorce each year.

• In about half of all marriages, one or both people have been married at least once before.

• In 1995, the groom's average age was 26.7; the bride's average age was 24.5. In 1960, the average age was 22.8 for the groom and 20.03 for the bride.

• Engagements last an average of nine months.

• The average U.S. wedding costs about $15,000.

• Approximately half of all marriages end in divorce.

• The average length of a marriage that ends in divorce is seven years.

Source: U.S. Bureau of the Census (1995).

Reasons for Marrying

Couples usually can give many positive reasons for getting married, but they often have difficulty identifying reasons not to marry. This section explores both a variety of positive characteristics that facilitate intimacy in marriage and also looks at some negative issues that can create problems in marriage.

Positive Reasons for Marrying

People marry for a number of positive reasons, here are a few that are important.

Companionship. Sharing one's life with someone is one common good reason for marriage. Companionship means having a partner with whom to share the journey of life. However, some people falsely assume that marriage will end loneliness. It seldom ends loneliness unless both partners feel good about themselves.

Love and intimacy. The need for love and intimacy is related to the need for companionship. Genuine affection for, and emotional connection with another can be a wonderful gift for both people.

Supportive partner. Another good reason for marriage is the opportunity it provides for growth as a human being and for nurturing your partner's growth. A marriage cannot survive if the partners think only of their own development, career concerns, or needs for recognition and accomplishment. But sharing each other's successes and genuinely supporting each other can enhance and stabilize a relationship. A mutual-admiration marriage has an excellent chance of success.

Sexual partner. Marriage has long been seen as a stable source of sexual satisfaction for both partners. As a result of the "sexual revolution," in the 1960's some people believed that sex and marriage did not necessarily have to go together. The AIDS epidemic, however, has again changed sexual attitudes to some degree. Marriage is once again often seen as a way to legitimize sexual feelings and behavior. But if sex is the major reason for marrying, the chance of the marriage surviving will not be very good.

Parenthood. Another traditional reason for marriage is to have children, but parenthood can be a mixed blessing. Most parents find that rearing children is a challenging and often frustrating task, but also a very satisfying one. When their children are grown and independent, most parents say that they have had enough parenting for one lifetime, but they also say that if they had it to do all over again, they would again decide to have children. Parenthood clearly is not for everyone: it can unite or divide a couple. Couples who successfully raise children together form important bonds between themselves and can be proud of what they accomplished together. Approached realistically, parenthood remains a very sound reason for marriage.

Negative Reasons for Marrying

There are also a number of poor reasons for getting married. Unless these issues are dealt with before marriage, they can create considerable challenges for a couple.

Premarital pregnancy. "Having to get married" because of premarital pregnancy is not a good way to go into marriage. Although the partners have shared sex, they may not have developed other aspects of true intimacy and may lack a real understanding of who they are marrying. Sex partners are not necessarily best friends or good marriage partners.

Rebellion against parents. Although many people are uncomfortable admitting that conflict with parents is a reason for marrying, it too often is the case. Marriage as a rebellion against repressive parents or a dysfunctional family may seem to be a rational option for a young person. People who have suffered in the crossfire of long-term conflicts between their parents are ready to leave home. People who have been the victims of parental alcohol or drug abuse or of physical, emotional, or sexual abuse all have legitimate reasons to flee their families.

But a legitimate reason for leaving your family is not necessarily a legitimate reason for getting married. It is better to develop personal independence and to come to terms with your family before thinking about marriage. Otherwise you run the risk of leaving one disastrous situation only to enter into another. Many who have fled parental abuse find they have "escaped" into an abusive marriage.

Seeking Independence. Closely related to the need to escape or rebel is the need to be independent. Young adults have a drive to succeed on their own. But becoming independent from your family is something that only you can do. You cannot rely on your partner to do it for you. Becoming independent takes years and is something you develop as you function more on your own.

AWARE it∈M 3.
Getting married is a good way to establish independence
from your family. (False)

The rebound. The rebound syndrome—recovering from a failed earlier relationship—is another negative reason for getting married. It is also one that is easier to detect in other people than in ourselves. The common reply to someone's warning is "Oh, no! I understand what you're saying, but this relationship is *different.*"

We tend to frame new relationships in positive terms, focusing on the joys and ignoring the fact that we may be reacting against a previous relationship. People on the rebound may "need" the new partner for emotional support. A marriage works better, however, when two people "want" rather than "need" each other. A rebound relationship is in danger from the start because the object of affection is seen not only as a friend or lover, but also as a counselor or healer of wounds of the old relationship.

Family or social pressure. Some families put subtle pressure on young people who do not marry by their late twenties. Both males and females may be pressured, but women often feel more pressure as they reach their late twenties. Many students who go away to college find that the classmates whom they left behind in their hometown are soon married and pregnant. People who choose for many good reasons not to marry young or who choose not to marry at all should not succumb to this pressure. Feeling rushed to be married is unlikely to produce a happy relationship.

Economic security. Although economic security has been a traditional reason for marrying, it has few merits today. With half or more of today's marriages likely to end in divorce, young people simply cannot afford to be dependent financially on their spouses.

There is also the genuine possibility that one or both spouses will become unemployed over the course of a marriage. Many people experience the trauma of being out of work for an extended period. Marriage does not automatically produce economic security, but couples continue to search for this within marriage. Financial problems are the most common marital problem Americans cite in national polls.

In summary, there are many positive and negative reasons for marrying, and people in love are often not objective when it comes to analyzing their own motives and actions. Being rational and realistic about reasons for marrying is not easy. But people who marry mainly for positive reasons are more likely to have a happier marriage than those whose marriage is based on negative reasons. For warning signs of potential marriage problems, see Box 3-2.

Box 3-2.

Warning Signs of a Problem Marriage

Monica McGoldrick, an eminent family therapist, has compiled the following list of warning signs of a problem marriage. She observes that the more characteristics that are true, the higher the potential for marital problems.

1. The couple meets or marries shortly after a significant loss.

2. The wish to distance from one's family-of-origin is a factor in the marriage.

3. The family backgrounds of each spouse are significantly different (religion, education, social class, ethnicity, age of the partners).

4. The spouses come from incompatible sibling constellations.

5. The couple resides either extremely close to or at a great distance from their family-of-origin.

6. The couple is dependent on either extended family financially, physically, or emotionally.

7. The couple marries before age 20.

8. The couple marries after an acquaintanceship of less than six months or after more than three years of engagement.

9. The wedding occurs without family or friends present.

10. The wife becomes pregnant before marriage or within the first year of marriage.

11. Either spouse considers her or his childhood or adolescence an unhappy time.

12. Either spouse has a poor relationship with siblings or parents.

13. Marital partners in either extended family were unstable.

Source: Adapted from "The Joining of Families Through Marriage: The New Couple" (p. 231) by M. McGoldrick. In *The Changing Family Life cycle: A Framework for Family Therapy* (2nd ed.) by B. Carter and M. McGoldrick, 1989, New York: Gardner Press. Copyright © 1989 by Allyn & Bacon. Reprinted by permission.

Does Living Together Prepare Couples for Marriage?

For many people, marriage is no longer considered a requirement for living with a romantic partner—that is, for living together. *Living together* is defined by the federal government as two unrelated adults of the opposite sex sharing the same living quarters.

It is clearly safe to say that living together is becoming more common in America. It is also true that living together has sparked a good deal of controversy. Numerous studies have been conducted to evaluate this phenomenon and to try to shed new light on the controversy surrounding living together. The results of these studies generally show that living together is not a good way to prepare for marriage.

Marriage is a risky proposition. Conflict is inevitable, and the likelihood of divorce is high. For these and numerous other reasons, more people are deciding to live together rather than marry. But living together is not necessarily good preparation for a successful marriage.

Types of Living Together Relationships

People live together for many reasons and have various types of living together arrangements. Researchers have identified four common patterns of living together: Linus blanket, emancipation, convenience, and testing.

Linus blanket. Named after the Linus character in the comic strip "Peanuts" who carries a security blanket with him, the Linus blanket relationship occurs when one partner is so dependent or insecure that he or she prefers a relationship with anyone to being alone. The insecure partner often finds the open communication on which a successful relationship thrives to be difficult. The stronger partner does not feel that he or she can criticize the more "fragile" partner. When the relationship ends, the insecure partner's fragile self-esteem falls even lower, and the departing partner feels guilty.

Emancipation. Some people use living together as a way to break free from their parents' values and influence. But because these people do not feel independent, they often enter into another living together relationship. The partner in this type of situation suffers because the individual seeking freedom brings too much unfinished business to the relationship and is trying to gain independence at another's expense.

Convenience. Relationships in which one person is the giver and the other is the taker are often relationships of convenience. Cohabiting relationships of this type may involve a man who is in the relationship to have a housewife (although some may live together for economic, sexual, and social reasons also). The woman supplies loving care and domestic labor—and hopes, but dares not ask, for marriage. When all is said and done, the man has taken but not given much in return and the woman has learned not to expect much from men.

Testing. Some people see living together as a true testing ground for marriage. If both partners are relatively mature and clearly committed to trying out living together, it can resemble marriage in some ways but it lacks the commitment of marriage.

In some ways, living together is just as complicated a relationship as marriage. But living together is not marriage nor is it good preparation for marriage.

Legal Issues in Living Together

A couple living together are not legally married. Marriage is a legal contract, and living together usually is not. Couples should consider the legal issues carefully before starting to live together.

As long as the living together goes well, there is not a whole lot to worry about. But what about deciding to separate and not live together? People who live together are no more stable in their relationships than married people; in fact, they are less stable. So when a couple living together breaks up, they have many issues to resolve. Problems can arise in the areas of personal property and income earned while living together.

Not too long ago, unmarried couples who were living together could end their relationship without legal hassles. But today many lawyers advise couples who wish to cohabit to draw up a legal agreement to protect themselves. If the relationship ends, the agreement serves as a guide for the rational and orderly division of property. The document should cover such issues as future earnings, who will receive custody of any offspring, and who will pay child support.

Living Together and Couple Satisfaction

In general, living together is not the best way to prepare people for marriage. It may be useful for some; for others, it is not a positive experience.

One study of 4,271 engaged couples found that couples living together had a less satisfying premarital relationship than engaged couples who lived apart (Figure 3-1). A total sample of 17,025 engaged couples completed a comprehensive premarital inventory called PREPARE, which evaluated their satisfaction in 14 aspects of the relationship. From the total sample, the most satisfied (numbering 2,124) and the least satisfied (numbering 2,147) were selected for comparison.

Of the couples selected (total = 4,271), about one-third (31 percent) were living together; in about another third (34 percent), one person lived with her or his parents and the other lived with other people. In one fifth (22 percent) of the couples, both partners lived with their parents and in only 13 percent of the couples did both partners live alone.

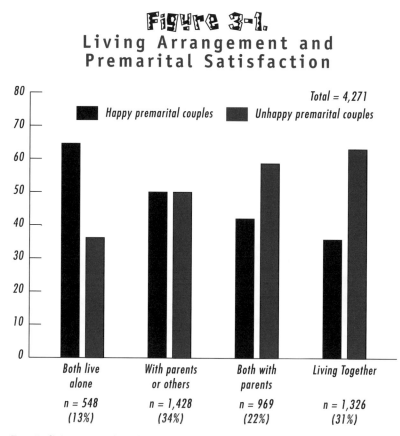

Figure 3-1.
Living Arrangement and Premarital Satisfaction

Total = 4,271

■ Happy premarital couples   ■ Unhappy premarital couples

Both live alone	With parents or others	Both with parents	Living Together
n = 548 (13%)	n = 1,428 (34%)	n = 969 (22%)	n = 1,326 (31%)

Source: From *Predicting Premarital Satisfaction on PREPARE Using Background Factors* by K. L. Stewart and D. H. Olson, (1990) (p.17), Life Innovations.

In this study, couples living together had the lowest level of premarital satisfaction, whereas premarital couples in which both people lived alone had the highest level of premarital satisfaction. Although about two-thirds of the couples living together fell into the low-satisfaction group, it also appears that engaged couples where both partners live alone are more satisfied than couples in which one or both partners still live with their parents.

One possible explanation for these findings is the way in which the partners became independent from their families-of-origin. Couples living together may be rebelling against their families to some degree. Couples in which both partners live with their parents might be too dependent on their parents. Those engaged couples in which both partners live alone might have achieved a more satisfactory degree of independence from their families-of-origin, and might therefore be happier with themselves and each other.

Another possible explanation for the findings is that high relationship satisfaction is common among people in love—before they actually move in together. The engaged couples who lived apart may not have had as many opportunities to get on each other's nerves. Couples living together may have less personal space, both physical and emotional. This intimacy makes it easier for conflicts to magnify and satisfactions to lessen.

Living Together as a Testing Ground for Marriage

Many couples assert that living together is a test of future marital compatibility, arguing that they would not consider marriage without first living with a potential mate. "The divorce rate is so high today," they argue, "I'm afraid of getting married before I know I'm absolutely sure."

The growing prevalence of living together among youth adds a new step in the mate selection process. Traditional courtship has been severely criticized by counselors because it emphasizes recreation and avoids conflictual issues. Also, the intensity of dating couples makes it possible for them to solve problems more easily. As one husband said in counseling, "When you're in love, you're willing to compromise on anything!"

Traditional courtship provides partners with idealized views of each other. This makes early marriage a period of difficult and sometimes severe adjustment for couples because they discover the unpleasant realities that have been masked during the dating and engagement period. Those who live together before marriage, some argue, will experience the realities of life together before they decide to "tie the knot."

Others object vigorously to living together on moral, religious, or philosophical grounds. Some see living together as inherently immoral. They argue that it violates religious beliefs. Another area of controversy is whether living together is a true testing ground for marriage. Because it is not truly a marriage, some argue, it cannot serve as a test of marriage. Living together is only "playing house," in the opinion of many observers. Finally, some argue that living together as a test of marriage really doesn't make much sense. To test marriage, they say, you need to actually get married.

Our society, for better or worse, is changing. Living together is becoming more common and more acceptable. Faced with the fear of divorce and the difficulty of marriage, people are trying to create new solutions to age-old problems. In the final analysis, however, there are no easy answers to the dilemmas we encounter in our intimate relationships. Later we will discuss some constructive ways to prepare for marriage.

AWARE item 4.
Living together before marriage (cohabiting) helps couples develop a more satisfying marriage. (False)

"To live is to love and to love is to live."
HAVELOCK ELLIS

Is Love Enough?

Listen to the radio or watch TV and it seems as if almost every songwriter is convinced that the answer to all of life's questions is *"love love love."* And couples in Western cultures commonly assume that being in love will be enough to keep their marriage happy forever. But to professionals who study marriage it is very clear that love is simply not enough to create a successful marriage.

AWARE item 5.
Love is all you need for a happy marriage. (False)

Love, unfortunately, is not a good predictor of whether a marriage will be successful. This is because almost all couples in the United States are in love when they marry—and yet at least half of them eventually get divorced.

AWARE item 6.
Love is a good predictor of whether a marriage will last. (False)

Predicting Marital Success

Researchers have invested an enormous amount of time and energy over many years trying to uncover the factors that lead to marital success, for this is a very important question to answer. As the late Dr. David R. Mace, once said, "Nothing in the world could make human life happier than to greatly increase the number of strong marriages." A strong marriage can be a wonderful foundation for a strong family. This is why researchers have worked so hard to understand and be able to predict marital success.

One of the most valuable findings researchers have made is that the quality of the premarital relationship is an excellent predictor of marital success. In simple terms, how two people get along before marriage is a fine indicator for how they will get along after marriage.

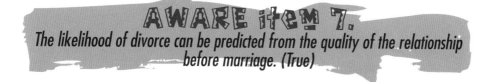

AWARE item 7.
The likelihood of divorce can be predicted from the quality of the relationship before marriage. (True)

Longitudinal research (research on the same group over an extended time period) is one good way to learn about marriage and family life. Instead of interviewing a couple or observing a family just once, it is very useful to follow family members over a long period of time. This gives researchers an idea of what stays the same and what changes in families. In studying predictors of marital success, a longitudinal study is useful because researchers can find out about a couple before marriage and then see how they do after marriage.

Two longitudinal studies using the PREPARE premarital inventory were able to predict, with about 80 to 85 percent accuracy, which couples were happily married and which got divorced. Here is how the researchers were able to do this: Two groups of engaged couples answered the PREPARE questions three to four months before their marriage and then were followed to a point three to four years after their marriage.

The PREPARE premarital inventory is a set of 165 questions that couples answer to identify the strengths in their relationship and also the areas where there are problems. The researchers found that on the basis of a couple's answers to the 165 questions, they could predict before the couple even got married whether they would end up happily married or divorced three to four years later. And they could predict the outcome accurately 80 to 85 percent of the time.

Relationship Characteristics That Predict a Happy Marriage

What are the key factors in predicting marital happiness? The researchers concluded that happy premarital couples—who generally tend to become happily married couples—are those who:

- *Have realistic expectations about the challenges of marriage.* Successful couples do not go into marriage starry-eyed and naive. They don't sugar coat the challenges of marriage and they recognize that the relationship will not always be perfectly smooth. Couples who succeed know if they work together they can create and maintain a strong marriage.

- *Communicate well.* The ability of partners to express themselves effectively to each other is critical to a successful relationship. Positive communication skills are probably the most important relationship skills that couples can learn to develop. See box 3-3 for two ways to build communication skills.

Box 3-3.

Daily Dialogue and Daily Compliments

Engaging in a Daily Dialogue and giving Daily Compliments are two ways of keeping a relationship exciting and healthy. These exercises may seem awkward at first, but the more you share your feelings, the easier it will become to do so.

The focus of the Daily Dialogue is your feelings about each other. Set aside five minutes a day and 15 minutes on the weekends to discuss:

- what you most enjoyed about your relationship that day
- what was dissatisfying about your relationship that day

Giving at least one Daily Compliment in your relationships helps focus on your strengths as individuals. It highlights the positive things about one another. Daily compliments prevent your relationship from becoming routine and make it more mutually satisfying.

Daily Dialogue and Daily Compliments are certainly not limited to marital relationships. These are skills that can improve any interpersonal relationship.

AWARE item 8.
Communication is the most useful and important skill couples can develop. (True)

- *Resolve conflicts well.* Disagreement is inevitable in any relationship. Couples don't agree on everything, but it is essential that they know (or learn) how to work through conflict successfully. Also resolving differences before marriage gives couples a greater chance for marital happiness later on.

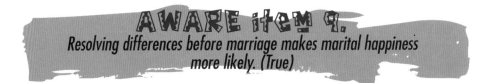
- *Feel good about the personality of their partner.* In simple terms, it is very important that you genuinely *like* the person you plan to marry. This person should be like your best friend and companion.
- *Agree on religious and ethical values.* Successful couples are united by shared beliefs and are in general agreement about religious values and beliefs. These shared values are an important foundation on which to build a strong and caring couple relationship.

- **Have egalitarian role relationships.** Happy couples balance responsibilities and power well. Partners respect each other's contributions to the good of the relationship, and share decision making fairly and openly. Each contributes ideas and leadership.

- **Balance individual and joint leisure activities.** Happy couples create a good balance between togetherness and separateness. They allow each other to develop personal interests and potentials because it is important to both individuals that they be the best they are capable of becoming. They encourage each other to have friendships and family relationships outside the partnership, because these other relationships also enrich their lives. Happy couples also find a satisfying amount of time to be together, doing relaxing and fun things or working on various projects.

If you can do these things well before marriage, studies of happy couples have shown that the likelihood of your doing them well after marriage is high. Couples who are skillful and happy before marriage are very likely to become skillful and happy married people.

~

Now go back to the beginning of the chapter and take the "Love and Marriage" AWARE Quiz again and see how you improved.

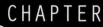

4 Preparing for Marriage

> " Failing to prepare is like preparing to fail. "

Aware Quiz

Are You Prepared?

Circle True or False

1 Couples prepare more for their wedding than for their marriage. T or F

2 Preparing for marriage should be just as important as planning for a career. T or F

3 Love is a poor predictor of who will stay married. T or F

4 Relationship skills come naturally and cannot be learned. T or F

5 A premarital program may bring up issues that would later become problems in marriage. T or F

6 The premarital inventory for couples called PREPARE can predict divorce with 80-85% accuracy. T or F

7 A good premarital program could help a couple decide not to get married. T or F

8 The family in which you grew up in has little impact on your marriage. T or F

9 The personality characteristics of the other person will bring out positive or negative traits in your own personality. T or F

10 You will have a unique couple relationship depending on the personality of the person you pair up with. T or F

Please complete the QUIZ before reading the chapter.

Marriage is Risky

More than 90 percent of all Americans marry at least once in their lifetime. The choice of who to marry is one of the most important decisions in life, affecting almost every aspect of your future. It seems odd that many people do not invest much time and energy preparing for their marriage compared to their wedding.

For couples marrying now, at least one of every two marriages is likely to end in divorce. Many married couples experience serious marital conflict early in their relationship, as evidenced by the high divorce rate early in marriage. In fact, the first year of marriage is the most dangerous year in terms of the likelihood of divorce, followed by the second year of marriage. Of those couples who end up divorcing, half do so in the first six years of marriage. So marriage is difficult for most couples and the risk of divorce is over 50 percent.

Is Getting Married Too Easy?

Getting married is easy. In fact, many observers believe it is too easy. But staying married is difficult. And staying happily married for a lifetime ranks, with parenthood, among the most challenging tasks in life.

Some people argue that it is too easy to get a divorce, implying that we should make divorce more difficult. Divorce is, in reality not all that easy, especially if there are children. But divorce is often a sad necessity, especially in marriages where the couple or family is hopelessly torn by emotional or physical abuse or the abuse of alcohol or other drugs.

We believe that a preventative approach to divorce is important. Rather than trapping people in unhappy marriages by making divorce more difficult, we should instead try to prevent the need for divorce. The real problem is that getting married is much too easy. It is certainly easier than getting a divorce. In this country getting into a bad marriage is much easier than getting out of one.

Getting a Marriage License Versus a Driver's License

In the United States, for example, it is easier to get a marriage license than a driver's license. To get a driver's license, you need to:

- Pass a written examination to demonstrate that you have accurate information about the rules and laws of driving.

- Pass a vision examination to demonstrate that you can see well.

- Pass a driving test to demonstrate that you have good driving skills.

To get a marriage license in most states, however, you simply fill out an application and pay a small fee. Then you can get married.

Poor driving habits cause untold physical and emotional damage in our society. But poor marriages and the resulting divorces also cause large amounts of injury and pain, causing much more damage each year than car accidents. We believe that there should be more requirements for getting married. To get a marriage license, a couple might be required to do the following:

- Pass a written examination to demonstrate that they have an accurate understanding of the qualities and abilities it takes to create and maintain a healthy marital relationship.

- Pass a vision examination to demonstrate that they have carefully developed a workable vision for their future family.

- Pass a practical test to demonstrate that they have good relationship skills in the areas of positive communication and conflict resolution.

Does this sound silly or overly idealistic? We don't think so. As family therapists we have counseled and interviewed hundreds of people who have experienced the devastation caused by poor marital and family relationships. If our society can create a reasonably good system for training new drivers, it certainly has the capacity to develop a reasonably good system for training new marital partners. The cost of neglecting this challenge is simply too great to ignore.

Plan for Marriage, Not Just Wedding

"Couples spend more time and money preparing for their wedding, which lasts a day, than for their marriage, which is intended to last a lifetime," David Olson points out. They often invest more energy in choosing a wedding cake, which will be gobbled down by hungry wedding guests in a few minutes, than they spend learning about the fundamental dynamics of marriage and how to improve their skills as partners. That is a big mistake.

Planning for the wedding often takes priority over preparing for marriage, but while getting married takes a few minutes, creating a successful marriage takes a lifetime. Getting married and staying married are two very different things. Couples should spend a lot more time preparing for the latter than for the former. It's a matter of getting your priorities straight. But because many couples don't do this, it is no surprise that the divorce rate is so high.

AWARE Item 1.
Couples prepare more for their wedding than for their marriage. (True)

Career Preparation and Marriage Preparation: A Comparison

How much time do people spend preparing for a job or career? The amount of time is often so large, we rarely add it up. But let's try. Say, for example, you want to be a teacher or an engineer. You go to preschool and elementary school and middle school and high school for many years to learn the basics: reading, writing, and arithmetic. Then, it's off to college for four or more years as you first continue your general education and then begin to concentrate in your specialty area. While you are in college you could do an internship, which gives you a chance to learn more about your planned profession by volunteering or working for limited pay with professionals in the field.

Finally, you get a job. You soon find that it is going to take many more years of work, study, and continuing education before you feel highly competent at your job and it develops into something more, a genuine career. Now you know beforehand that the path to developing a successful career will be long and challenging, but you make the important decision to go down that path because you understand in your heart that good things take time.

Contrast this very careful and dedicated approach to career development with how we tend to view preparation for marriage in American culture. First, people often date several people over a few years. Couples "fall in love" with each other and on the basis of "falling in love," they decide to get married.

Couples do not go to "marriage" school or even think about reading any books about marriage or visiting a counselor. Instead, the bride-to-be and her mother spend countless hours planning every detail of the wedding ceremony, usually with modest input from the groom-to-be. The big day arrives, the wedding ceremony is over in a very short time. The families have spent thousands of dollars for this event. And the couple go off alone, with little guidance or marriage education, to try to figure out what to do "till death do us part."

The fact that our society has chosen not to develop a meaningful system of marriage preparation for young people strikes us as a tragedy. Think about some well-known people in the news today. Consider the golfer Tiger Woods, the basketball player Michael Jordan, the first woman to become U.S. Secretary of State, Madeleine Albright. How good would they be at golf, basketball, or international diplomacy if they had prepared for their roles in the same hap-hazard way we train young people for marriage? Is society saying that golf, basketball, and international relations are more critical to its well-being than the development of good marriages and strong families?

R. Herbert Newton summed it up only too well when he said, "The dignity of a vocation is always to be measured by the seriousness of the preparation made for it. How then can we appraise marriage?" We hope that you will personally value your marriage more than society today apparently values marriage and family, and that you will honor your commitment to marriage by being as prepared as you possibly can—not only for a beautiful wedding but for a long and happy marriage.

AWARE item 2.
Preparing for marriage should be just as important as planning for a career. (True)

Love is Not Enough

You may be wondering, "Why do I have to prepare for marriage?" The answer is both complex and quite simple. Fairy-tale marriages are, unfortunately, just that—fictional. Happily-ever-after is attainable, but like anything else that is worthwhile in life, it requires a lot of commitment and effort from both partners. Couples who are in love want to believe in happily-ever-after, but entering into marriage without preparation is like entering a dance competition without learning the steps or playing in a symphony without ever taking music lessons. There are basic relationship skills you can learn that will greatly increase your chances of having a successful marriage.

We know that being in love is not enough because almost everyone that gets married is in love but over half get divorced. Close relationships are much too complex and challenging. Sailing through difficult times with love as your only armor makes for a dangerous ride. You need the anchor of love, but also a good foundation of compatibility, some life jackets in the form of external resources, a compass to help guide you and show you that you both want to sail in the same direction, and a mighty good pair of oars—coping resources—to get you through the storms.

In almost every other aspect of life, we prepare the most for the things that are the most important to us, the things that we are most committed to. Except for marriage. Somewhere along the way our society went off course, choosing to believe that love will lead the way, that love will get us through anything. But more than half of those who marry find themselves at a dead end or a lonely road and—after they have made a heavy emotional investment and often have brought children into the marriage—they divorce.

You can make better choices—choices that will help you select the best road to drive on. The street signs on that road will not be blurry, they will be clear and concise. The road will be well-lit. It is up to you. Which road would you rather take?

AWARE Item 3.
Love is a poor predictor of who will stay married. (True)

How Can Couples Prepare for Marriage?

People are not naturally experts at developing relationships any more than they are naturally experts at a profession. Fortunately, the skills required to build healthy relationships are skills that can be learned. You will read about and learn many of these in this book. Increasing your general knowledge about relationships, families and marriage will help you make better choices and develop quality relationships. You also will have a more realistic understanding of what you can and cannot expect from interpersonal relationships. Premarital programs can help couples learn to be realistic about marriage. Most programs also involve couple discussion on important relationship areas such as communication and conflict resolution. Premarital preparation can get a marriage off to a good start.

AWARE Item 4.
Relationship skills come naturally and cannot be learned. (False)

Effective premarital programs should involve a premarital inventory to assess the couple relationship. The inventory should focus on important couple issues such as personality, finances and parenting. These issues, if not addressed and dealt with before marriage, may eventually lead to problems in marriage. Effective premarital programs also should teach couples important relationship skills such as communication and conflict resolution. And, ideally, the premarital program will prime the couple for further couple enrichment.

Good educational programs for premarital couples should be more available. After the wedding, couples would also be well-advised to continue their education about marriage. They might read and discuss books on marriage, or they might attend marriage enrichment seminars or workshops as preventive maintenance.

AWARE Item 5.

A premarital program may bring up issues that would later become problems in marriage. (True)

What Is The PREPARE/ENRICH Program?

The PREPARE (PREmarital Personal and Relationship Evaluation) Program was created for couples who are in a committed relationship and thinking seriously about marrying. The PREPARE Program is designed for couples planning to marry. The ENRICH (Enriching and Nurturing Relationship Issues, Communication and Happiness) Program is designed for married couples seeking enrichment and counseling and couples who have cohabited for two or more years.

Both PREPARE and ENRICH Programs include first taking a 165-item Inventory designed to help couples examine their couple relationship so that they can build on their relationship strengths. Both programs are designed to help partners learn to share their feelings and ideas with one another and to help them learn how to work together to achieve their goals. The Program assists participants in identifying relationship areas they would like to enrich, build on each couple's strengths, and teach couples how to communicate more effectively with one another about a variety of important topics.

PREPARE Can Predict Divorce with 80% Accuracy

Perhaps the most impressive aspect of the PREPARE Couple Program is the high predictive validity. This means that PREPARE is able to predict before marriage with 80-85 percent accuracy who will be happily married and who will be divorced within three years of completing the inventory. The high accuracy level tells us that the quality of a couple's relationship before marriage is a very good measure of what will happen to the couple after marriage. Therefore, if we can improve the relationship before marriage, we can improve the marital relationship.

AWARE Item 6.
The premarital inventory for couples called PREPARE can predict divorce with 80-85% accuracy. (True)

Although PREPARE has proven to have high predictive validity, the inventory cannot be "passed" or "failed." It is simply a personalized assessment of the couple relationship. Some couples (10-15%), after taking PREPARE, decide not to marry. In these cases, the couples probably have saved themselves some heartache since research found their scores to be almost identical to couples who eventually divorce. Therefore, a good premarital inventory, such as PREPARE can help prevent divorce by defining a problematic relationship before marriage.

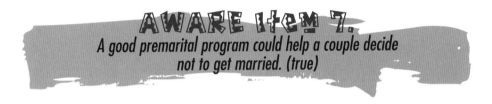

AWARE Item 7.
A good premarital program could help a couple decide not to get married. (true)

Twelve Major Areas in PREPARE/ENRICH Program

Theory and research on couples have identified the most important issues to focus on with couples, including: communication, conflict resolution, family-of-origin, finances, and goals. The PREPARE/ENRICH Program builds on these important areas. The twelve content areas are: Marriage Expectations, Personality Issues, Communication, Conflict Resolution, Financial Management, Leisure Activities, Idealistic Distortion, Sexual Relationship, Children and Parenting, Family and Friends, Role Relationship, and Spiritual Beliefs.

Marriage Expectations

Personality Issues

Communication

Conflict Resolution

Financial Management

Leisure Activities

Idealistic Distortion

Sexual Relationship

Children and Parenting

Family and Friends

Role Relationship

Spiritual Beliefs

Box 4-1.

Twelve Content Areas in PREPARE/ENRICH Program

Marriage Expectations assesses an individual's expectations about love, commitment, and conflicts in her/his relationship.

Personality Issues focuses on each individual's satisfaction with the personality characteristics of the partner as expressed through the partner's behavioral traits.

Communication measures each individual's beliefs, feelings, and attitudes toward the role of communication in the maintenance of her/his relationship.

Conflict Resolution evaluates an individual's attitudes, feelings, and beliefs about the existence and resolution of conflict in the relationship.

Financial Management focuses on attitudes and concerns about the way economic issues are managed within the couple's relationship.

Leisure Activities evaluates each individual's preferences for using free time.

Idealistic Distortion assesses the tendency of individuals to answer personal questions in a socially desirable manner.

Sexual Relationship assesses an individual's feelings and concerns about affection and the sexual relationship with her/his partner.

Children and Parenting measures an individual's attitudes and feelings about having and raising children.

Family and Friends assesses feelings and concerns about relationships with relatives, in-laws, and friends.

Role Relationship evaluates an individual's beliefs, attitudes, and feelings about marital and family roles.

Spiritual Beliefs assesses attitudes, feelings, and concerns about the meaning of religious beliefs and practices within the context of the relationship.

Family-of-Origin Issues

When we marry, we not only marry another person but also, metaphorically speaking, marry that person's family. Because of the importance of the family-of-origin (the family in which we grew up) in shaping our view of the world and expectations for a relationship, the inventory also focuses on the family-of-origin. Partners describe their couple relationship and their family-of-origin in terms of closeness and flexibility on the inventory (Box 4-2). There are two scales focusing on family-of-origin issues (Family Closeness and Family Flexibility), and two scales focusing on the couple's relationship (Couple Closeness and Couple Flexibility). The four descriptions are then plotted on a Couple and Family Map, which focuses on closeness and flexibility in couples and families.

AWARE Item 8.
The family in which you grew up in has little impact on your marriage. (False)

The goal of this part of the inventory is to help the couple see the importance of their family-of-origin relationship in their couple relationship. This helps the couple learn to better understand how they bring (or will bring) the communication patterns and beliefs they learned in their family-of-origin into their marriage. Also, the couple may have disagreements because they come from very different families of origin.

It also helps the couple be more proactive in thinking about what they want to bring and do not want to bring from their family-of-origin into their couple relationship. Instead of waiting until disagreements arise, the couple can learn about their inevitable differences ahead of time and can plan together to prevent their differences from becoming more serious relationship problems.

Four Family-of-Origin and Couple Areas

Closeness:

The Couple and Family Closeness areas describe the level of emotional closeness experienced among family members and the degree to which members balance togetherness and separateness.

Couple Closeness assesses closeness in the couple's current relationship. **Family Closeness** measures closeness in the families-of-origin.

Flexibility:

The Couple and Family Flexibility areas measure the ability of a couple to change and be flexible when necessary. Items deal with leadership issues and the ability to switch responsibilities and change rules when needed.

Couple Flexibility evaluates the flexibility in couple's current relationship. **Family Flexibility** assesses patterns of change in the families-of-origin.

(For more details on Family-of-Origin, see Chapter 13)

Personality:

Four personality areas are assessed in the Inventories: Assertiveness, Self-Confidence, Avoidance, and Partner Dominance. *Assertiveness* evaluates a person's ability to express his/her feelings to the partner and to be able to ask for what she/he would like. *Self-Confidence* measures how good a person feels about himself/herself and the person's ability to control things in his/her life. *Avoidance* evaluates a person's tendency to minimize issues and reluctance to deal with issues directly. *Partner Dominance* assesses how much a person feels the partner tries to control him/her and dominates her/his life.

There is a positive cycle linking assertiveness and self confidence and a negative cycle linking avoidance and partner dominance (See Figure 4-1). In the positive cycle, as a person uses more assertiveness, their level of self confidence tends to increase. As a person's self confidence increases, their willingness and ability to be more assertive increases. In the negative cycle, when one person perceives the partner as dominating, a common reaction is for that person to avoid dealing with issues. As one person uses more avoidance, the other person will tend to become more dominant.

Figure 4-1.

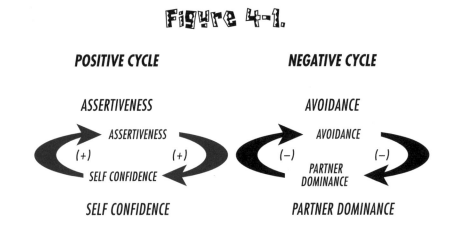

POSITIVE CYCLE	NEGATIVE CYCLE

ASSERTIVENESS

AVOIDANCE

ASSERTIVENESS

AVOIDANCE

(+) (+)

(−) (−)

SELF CONFIDENCE

PARTNER DOMINANCE

SELF CONFIDENCE

PARTNER DOMINANCE

The personality assessment of the PREPARE/ENRICH Program is designed to increase the couple's understanding of each partner and how these personality characteristics are related to the couple relationship. The individual personalities combine to create a very unique couple relationship. You most likely have had this experience in friendships and other interpersonal relationships. You probably feel differently about yourself depending on who you are interacting with. This is because other people's personalities will emphasize different aspects of your personality. In a couple relationship, this influence is usually even stronger. This is one of the reasons why it is so important to choose a partner whose personality you like, someone who brings out characteristics of yourself that you like, and someone with whom you create a positive 'couple personality.'

AWARE Item 10.

You will have a unique couple relationship depending on the personality of the person you pair up with. (True)

Six Couple Exercises in the PREPARE/ENRICH Program

If you were participating in the PREPARE/ENRICH Couple Program you and your partner would complete these six couple goals and exercises with the focus on your couple relationship. These goals and exercises have been integrated into various chapters and exercises of the BUILDING RELATIONSHIPS book. You will have the opportunity to practice these skills with other relationships, including your peers and parents.

1. Explore relationship strength and growth areas. Couples choose 3 relationship strengths and 3 relationship growth areas from the 12 PREPARE/ENRICH areas. Strengths and growth areas are discussed independently and as a couple.

2. Strengthen couple communication skills, including assertiveness and active listening. Couples create a 'Wish List' and use Assertiveness and Active Listening skills in sharing their Wish Lists with one another. You will have the opportunity to learn about and practice your assertiveness and active listening skills in Chapter 7: Communication Skills.

3. Resolve couple conflict using the Ten-Step Procedure. Couples use a conflict resolution model to guide them in solving a problem or disagreement. You will also have the chance to use the Ten-Step Procedure to resolve a problem or issue in your life in Chapter 8: Conflict Resolution Skills.

4. Explore family-of-origin issues using the Couple and Family Map. Couples evaluate both their family-of-origin and their couple relationship in terms of closeness and flexibility. You will discover where your family operates on the Family Map if you do the exercise in Chapter 13: Understanding Your Family.

5. Develop a workable budget and financial plan. Couples develop a budget and establish long-term and short-term financial goals. You also will create a budget and think about your financial goals in Chapter 11: Financial Decisions.

6. Develop personal, couple, and family goals. Couples develop an Action Plan for their personal, couple and family goals. You will also define some goals in Chapter 12: Values, Beliefs & Behaviors.

~

Now that you have completed this chapter on preparing for marriage, why don't you go back and respond to the AWARE scale once more. See how you're doing.

5 Adjusting to Marriage

> **There is hardly any activity, any enterprise, which is started with such tremendous hopes and expectations and which fails so regularly as love.**
>
> DR. ERICH FROMM, PSYCHIATRIST

MARRIAGE

Aware Quiz

Marriage Challenges

Circle True or False

1 Marriage might be disappointing and frustrating at first.　　　　T or F

2 Love, for an engaged couple, is often different than
love for married couples.　　　　T or F

3 Romantic love tends to fade after marriage.　　　　T or F

4 The first two years of marriage are usually the best.　　　　T or F

5 People are more willing to change their habits to please their
partner after marriage than before.　　　　T or F

6 After marriage, it is easier to accept a partner's habits
that bother you.　　　　T or F

7 The opinions of family and friends will have little effect on
marital success and satisfaction.　　　　T or F

8 Old personal relationships can interfere with the
couple relationship.　　　　T or F

9 Getting married will help ensure that you will not feel
bored or lonely.　　　　T or F

10 Adjusting to marriage is easier if your partner is also
your best friend.　　　　T or F

*Please complete the QUIZ
before reading the chapter.*

Newlyweds: The Difficult Adjustment

Marriage is a more difficult transition than most couples anticipate. This is true even for couples who are well prepared for marriage and feel very good about their relationship. Many couples expect that marriage will be easy and that it will be similar to what they have experienced with each other before marriage.

AWARE item 1.
Marriage might be disappointing and frustrating at first. (True)

Operating As a Couple Is Hard

The newlywed stage, roughly the first two years of marriage, is a difficult transition for couples because the partners must put some space between their families-of-origin, give up their previous independence, and begin to function as a couple. Many individuals are disappointed to learn that this does not happen easily and without stress.

How do I love thee?

Americans virtually have only one word to describe an infinite range of feelings. Love. People claim to love football teams, pets, ice cream, cars and people. It is not surprising, then, that the word "love" cannot have one universal definition. In fact, entire books have been written trying to explain love.

Love contains many elements including: passion, romance, respect, jealousy, support, commitment, friendship and tenderness. Dating and married couples can both experience many different qualities of love, but there are common distinctions. Love for dating and engaged couples typically contains more physical attraction, intimacy and passion while love for married couples tends to contain more commitment and affection.

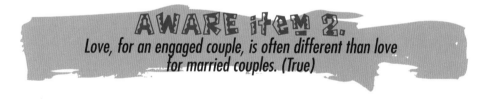

AWARE item 2.
Love, for an engaged couple, is often different than love for married couples. (True)

"Young love is a flame; very pretty, very hot and fierce, but still only light and flickering. The love of the older and disciplined heart is as coals, deep-burning, unquenchable."
-- HENRY WARD BEECHER

Love Changes over Time

It is normal for the intensity and passion of a relationship to change over time. It is very common for the intensity of a relationship to diminish dramatically after marriage. In marriage we live so close together that we get used to—and even get bored with one another. Frankly, if we were passionately in love all the time, we would soon be so exhausted that we could not function in the real world.

AWARE item 3.
Romantic love tends to fade after marriage. (True)

One important study of newlyweds found that about half the couples doubted that their marriage would last because they were already experiencing significant marital problems during the first year. About 40 percent of the individuals in the study found marriage harder than they had expected it would be, and noted that their partner had become more critical of them after marriage.

Although many people believe the early years of marriage are the best, the fact is that adjusting to one another is difficult for most people. The divorce rate is actually higher the first couple years of marriage than in later stages. The image of two lovebirds happily bedded down in their love nest is often inaccurate.

AWARE item 4.
The first two years of marriage are usually the best. (False)

Marriage Will Not Change Your Partner

One of the major reasons newlywed couples find the adjustment to marriage so difficult is that they typically are too idealistic. Premarital relationships are often filled with fantasies and myths, especially the notion that the partner's undesirable traits will change after the couple is married.

Unfortunately, marriage neither changes people nor makes it easier for others to change them. In fact, marriage often magnifies undesirable traits. A person who arrives late for a date or other activities before marriage will typically arrive late after marriage. A person who is sloppy before marriage will be sloppy after marriage—but the sloppiness will become more evident and problematic after marriage.

Marriage doesn't change people, in fact, undesirable traits may become even more apparent in the closeness of marriage. One young woman told of a serious problem which began before marriage. She reported that her fiance was kind and gentle with her until the night before the wedding. Then, he became angry and shoved her in an argument over the cost of the ceremony. She thought he did this because he was tense about the upcoming ceremony, so she went through with the wedding. In the first six months of their marriage, her husband physically abused her on eight separate occasions, with the severity of the abuse increasing as the months passed. She divorced her husband after one year of marriage.

Box 5-1 focuses on how pleasant premarital fantasies can become disturbing marital realities.

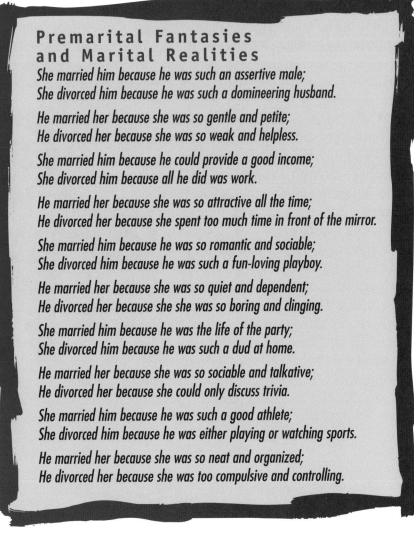

Box 5-1.

Premarital Fantasies and Marital Realities

She married him because he was such an assertive male;
She divorced him because he was such a domineering husband.

He married her because she was so gentle and petite;
He divorced her because she was so weak and helpless.

She married him because he could provide a good income;
She divorced him because all he did was work.

He married her because she was so attractive all the time;
He divorced her because she spent too much time in front of the mirror.

She married him because he was so romantic and sociable;
She divorced him because he was such a fun-loving playboy.

He married her because she was so quiet and dependent;
He divorced her because she she was so boring and clinging.

She married him because he was the life of the party;
She divorced him because he was such a dud at home.

He married her because she was so sociable and talkative;
He divorced her because she could only discuss trivia.

She married him because he was such a good athlete;
She divorced him because he was either playing or watching sports.

He married her because she was so neat and organized;
He divorced her because she was too compulsive and controlling.

From Compliments to Criticisms

In one of life's puzzles, partners often become more critical and less accepting of each other after marriage. When we love and marry someone, our love should ensure a certain amount of respect and civility in the relationship. But we often treat strangers on the street and friends with more respect and tolerance than we do our partner.

It is almost as if a marriage license becomes a license to be impolite and sometimes mean. This is probably a function of the fact that close living and frustration go hand in hand. Because you become more aware of your partner's habits and see them more often, it becomes harder to accept a partner's habits that bother you. But healthy and happy relationships are based on kindness and generosity.

AWARE item 6.

After marriage, it is easier to accept a partner's habits that bother you. (False)

External Factors That Affect the Couple Relationship

A marriage is not isolated from other aspects of our lives. Though couples sometimes wish they could run off together and live in a world all by themselves (say on a beautiful deserted island) this is not realistic. Marriage is open to the world and all its influences. A marriage is affected by the external environment; by the couple's extended families, friends, the working world, and society as a whole. Besides these external influences, each partner has an internal environment—the thoughts and feelings carried deep inside each person. We also bring our internal environment into the couple relationship, for better or for worse. So marriage is open and affected by countless aspects of the world in which you live.

Parents' Opinions Predict Couple Satisfaction

Parents, friends, the mass media, and countless other forces affect the couple as they adjust to one another. Parents are especially influential. Although most couples love and appreciate their parents, some couples fantasize about running away from their families-of-origin. They may want to create a new life together free of all the usual well-meaning advice from parents. This comment from one newlywed woman reflects that frustration:

> It gets unbearable sometimes, you know? His mom is always giving me ideas on how to cook just how he likes it. She doesn't realize that our marriage is really different from their marriage. I'm not a very good cook, and Bill does most of the cooking. His mom acts like I'm going to destroy her son if I don't know how to make all his favorite foods.

There are many areas, however, in which listening carefully to parents' ideas can prove very useful. It's not necessary to agree with all their opinions, but understanding what parents are saying is important in making wise decisions. One study of 5,174 engaged couples showed that when both sets of parents were not happy about the couple's plans to marry, nearly 88 percent of the couples had a low level of couple satisfaction. Among engaged couples where only one set of parents was negative about the upcoming marriage, almost 73 percent of the couples had a low level of satisfaction with their relationship. On the other hand, when both sets of parents were positive about the couple's premarital relationship, almost 58 percent of the couples had a high level of relationship satisfaction. See Figure 5-1 for the details of this study with 5,174 engaged couples.

Figure 5-1.

Couple's Satisfaction Compared with Parents' Reaction to the Upcoming Marriage (Total = 5,174)

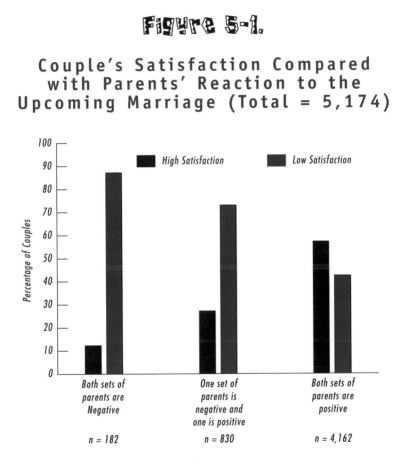

This study shows that parents are likely to sense trouble in their children's premarital relationships. If the parents are not positive about the relationship and the couple is not really satisfied either, then it would be wise for the couple to sit down and talk about the situation. The couple might also find it helpful to talk with their parents about what is happening. This is a very difficult thing to do and it can be painful to open our relationships to others for examination. But, not trying to work out problems before marriage can lead to genuine disaster after marriage.

Past Relationships Are Likely to Change

When a couple marries, the partner's existing friendships and past relationships may cause fear and jealousy in the partner. It is likely that these past relationships will change after marriage. Newlyweds often complain about how perturbed their partner gets when they simply want to go out with "the boys" to play basketball or to spend time with an "old girlfriend" over lunch. The need to maintain old friendships needs to be discussed carefully and cautiously between partners. On the one hand, it is reasonable for both partners to want to maintain existing friendships. Besides, we would soon be pretty bored with each other if we spent all our time alone together.

On the other hand, if a spouse feels left out or neglected because of old friendships, trouble can arise. The underlying factor is fear, even though individuals may have a hard time admitting it. We fear that we will be left out and the friendships will be more important than the marriage. The couple needs to discuss all of this honestly and openly and work out a balance between the marriage and other friendships.

Even more difficult to deal with than existing friendships are relationships with ex-lovers. Jealousy stemming from fear is especially common when a partner maintains a relationship—even a platonic friendship—with an ex-lover. Honest communication between spouses is the solution, but anyone will tell you this is not easy. For example, one man commented about his wife:

> *She wants to have lunch with Joseph to talk about what's happening in their lives. She says she wants to tell him how happy she is in her marriage with me. She says they were good friends for so long it's important to stay friends. She knows he will be happy for us. And she wants to hear about his life with Sarah and their two daughters. She says it's just friendship, and what's wrong with friendship? But I'm not so sure.*

Sometimes the friend of a spouse becomes a friend to the partner, although this is unlikely if the friend is an ex-lover. Likewise, when someone is friends with a couple, that person's partner may also develop a friendship with the couple. In many other cases though, these friendships simply do not develop.

Marriages are fragile relationships. We have to be very careful not to do anything that would be hurtful or threatening to our partner. This may mean that some existing personal friendships and relationships may cool over time. Although we may value these relationships, they can sometimes cause pain and conflict in marriage.

AWARE item 8.
Old personal relationships can interfere with the couple relationship. (True)

Marriage Does Not Erase Loneliness and Boredom

In our society we tend to be unrealistic about marriage. We sometimes put marriage on a high pedestal, creating such an idealistic dream that the reality of marriage can never compete with our fantasies. We are just as likely to criticize marriage, making fun of it for its failings and the fact that even the best of relationships are far from perfect.

The Nobel Prize-winning Colombian novelist Gabriel García Márquez clearly knows a strong marriage when he sees one. In his powerful novel *Love in the Time of Cholera,* he depicts a 72-year-old widow, Fermina Daza, pondering her long-term marriage, which has just ended with the accidental death of her husband:

> *She was lost in her longing to understand. She could not conceive of a husband better than hers had been, and yet when she recalled their life she found more difficulties than pleasures, too many mutual misunderstandings, useless arguments, unresolved angers. Suddenly she sighed: "It is incredible how one can be happy for so many years in the midst of so many squabbles, so many problems, damn it, and not really know if it was love or not."*

We think Fermina's marriage was, indeed, full of love. But people are so puzzled over what love and marriage are really all about that they often get depressed over the fact that *real* love doesn't look like love in the movies. Real love stories contain elements of both "good" and "bad" moments. But most people only tell others about romantic moments and exaggerate how much fun love is.

A *real* marriage does not solve every problem and satisfy every need in 30 minutes like a TV sitcom. Before marriage, every human being gets bored and feels lonely, at least occasionally. Likewise, after marriage we still get bored—with life in general and also with our marriage. And we feel lonely, isolated, and alienated from other people. Everyone feels this way sometimes, even in a good marriage. The key is to realize that these are perfectly normal feelings both before and after marriage. We need to learn how to develop trust in our marriage and how to reach out to one another for support and comfort. We will talk about this a great deal more, especially in the chapter on communication.

AWARE item 9.
Getting married will help ensure that you will not feel bored or lonely. (False)

Internal Factors That Enhance the Couple Relationship

We have told you that a host of external factors influence marriage, for better and worse. Much of our discussion has focused on negative issues: the fact that parents and other family members can seem bothersome sometimes, the fact that after marriage partners may find old friendships and relationships dying out; and the fact that marriage does not necessarily cure boredom and loneliness.

Besides these external influences on marriage, we each bring the thoughts and feelings deep inside us to the relationship. Love tends to magnify our imperfections as well as our partner's, which makes it a prime place to experience annoyance and fear. Allow yourself to experience these feelings, knowing they are a normal part of love. Accept your feelings and, through communication, they can increase closeness in your relationship. We often assume we should just know how to love. The truth is that love is a constant and conscious process of learning.

Our internal world is influenced by our external world, and what is inside us influences how we relate to our partner. Marriage is affected by many elements in the world. If we stay optimistic, we can adapt successfully to the external world and create a good marriage in spite of the difficulties we face. A positive attitude is essential in creating a sound marital relationship.

What keeps a marriage going? Robert and Jeanette Lauer surveyed 351 couples. They asked husbands and wives to rank the important aspects of a good marriage. What is especially interesting about the Lauers' research is the amount of agreement they found between husbands and wives in rating the important factors. As you can see in Box 5-2, the husbands' rankings are remarkably close to the wives' rankings. In fact, the top seven factors are exactly the same for husbands and wives.

Box 5-2.

What Keeps a Marriage Going:

	Ranking	
	Husbands	Wives
My spouse is my best friend.	1	1
I like my spouse as a person.	2	2
Marriage is a long-term commitment.	3	3
Marriage is sacred.	4	4
We agree on aims and goals.	5	5
My spouse has grown more interesting.	6	6
I want the relationship to succeed.	7	7
An endearing marriage is important to social stability.	8	10
We laugh together.	9	8
I am proud of my spouse's achievements.	10	15
We agree on a philosophy of life.	11	9
We agree about our sex life.	12	14
We agree on how and how often to show affection.	13	10

Let's look at three very important factors: friendship, a pleasing personality, and enjoying time together.

My Partner Is My Best Friend

The couples in the Lauers' study rated friendship as essential to a good marriage. "My spouse is my best friend." Many husbands and wives agreed to the statement. Romantic love may provide the sparks that ignite a couple to get married, but genuine friendship has a lot more staying power than passion. Over the long haul, friendship is a very important aspect of marriage.

I Like My Partner's Personality

The couples in the Lauers' study genuinely liked one another. It may seem hard to believe, but people who really do not like each other sometimes still do marry one another. Some people marry for the right reasons, but some marry for the wrong reasons. Individuals sometimes get married because of factors like a premarital pregnancy or pressure from their family, even though they know deep down that they simply do not find anything very pleasing about their partner's personality. These marriages have a big strike against them from the start.

We Enjoy Time Together

The successfully married couples in the Lauers' study also enjoyed spending time with one another. They liked doing things together and had many similar interests. Again, getting married for the right reasons can make it much easier to adjust to marriage. Marrying for the wrong reasons can make the adjustment to marriage very difficult.

AWARE item 10.
Adjusting to marriage is easier if your partner is also your best friend. (True)

Now that you have finished reading Chapter 5 on Adjusting to Marriage, why don't you answer the ten questions at the beginning of this chapter (AWARE Quiz—Marriage Challenges) and see how much your score has improved.

Marriage

ation

Family

Value

" **Parenthood is much easier to get into than out of.**

BRUCE LANSKY, author of
Mother Murphy's Laws (1986) "

Love   Value   Dating

Children

Finances

Challenges

Aware Quiz

Parenting Challenges

Circle True or False

1 Most couples agree on the number of children they want
and when to have them.   T or F

2 Having children will dramatically change your life.   T or F

3 Having children can have a negative effect on a couple's marriage.   T or F

4 Taking care of children can be stressful, with little reward.   T or F

5 Raising children is a natural activity that requires little training.   T or F

6 Most couples equally share parenting responsibilities.   T or F

7 Most fathers are actively involved in their children's lives.   T or F

8 Most couples agree on how best to discipline their children.   T or F

9 Each child costs about $100,000 to raise.   T or F

10 Marital conflict can have a negative effect on children.   T or F

*Please complete the QUIZ
before reading the chapter.*

Parenthood: Choice vs. Chance

Parenthood is the most difficult, the most satisfying, and the most important job in the world. It may also be the only job that does not require some form of organized training. There is no greater responsibility or challenge in life than raising a child. For many people there is also no greater satisfaction. The ideal is to raise children to be independent enough to eventually care for themselves but connected enough to look to their family for guidance, support, and companionship. The ideal is neither complete independence nor complete dependence, but a happy medium that we can call interdependence.

Many people criticize parenthood, focusing only on the negative aspects of the parental role. Others—especially those who are not parents yet—romanticize parenthood, focusing only on its rewards. They think about having a cute little baby who's sweet, cuddly and always lovable. But in reality, parenting can be a very demanding, frustrating, and thankless job. It can also be a severe drain on your energy, finances, and time.

Parenting is also the most exciting and fulfilling thing you could ever do. Creating a human being together with your mate is truly a miracle. When parents in their fifties and sixties, looked back over their many years of parenthood, they generally felt it had been a rewarding process. From the vantage point that age and experience gives them, the satisfactions for these veteran parents have been many. But ask them if they would like to do it again, starting today, and they are likely to chuckle: *Are you kidding? I wouldn't take a million dollars for the experience I had of being a mother [or father]. It was very rewarding. But all the money in the world wouldn't be enough to get me to do it again. Now that it's over and I have some time, and money and freedom. I'm into a new stage in life."* Talk with your own parents and grandparents about all this.

In this chapter, we'll look frankly at the realities of parenthood, at the good times and the difficult times. We'll emphasize how individuals can learn to be successful dads and moms and enjoy the process. But we will not urge you to become a parent any more than we would suggest you not have children. Each person has to decide this issue for herself or himself.

It is important that people make rational choices about becoming parents, rather than leaving it up to chance. It's important that before they marry, couples talk about critical issues: if they genuinely want to be parents, when they believe it would be best to become parents, and how many children they would like to have.

Unfortunately, couples usually don't discuss children before marriage, so they have no idea whether they agree or disagree on this subject. Perhaps it doesn't cross their minds that these would be important things to talk about. For whatever reason, a high percentage of people stumble into parenthood accidentally or without much thought. So most couples do not talk about whether they want children, when they should have them and the number they would like.

AWARE item 1.
Most couples agree on the number of children they want and when to have them. (False)

Recent estimates indicate that about half of all births in the United States result from unintentional pregnancies. The problem is that unintentional pregnancy is a very difficult way to begin the life-long responsibility of parenthood.

In our society, we try to carefully plan our education and career to create as good a working life as possible for ourselves. We tend to spend a lot of time picking out an automobile, debating and reviewing the finer points of make, model, engine size, color, and other features. A bride may compare the pros and cons of dozens of wedding dresses, examining the tiniest details of each dress. Clearly, we are a planning-oriented society. Yet when it comes to having children, we often stumble into it, throwing caution to the winds. Box 6-1 provides a list of 10 ridiculous ideas that lead to unwanted parenthood.

It has been argued that the greatest gift a mother and father can give their child is a good marriage. A good marriage promises a child support and stability and provides a model of family love that, as an adult, the child can follow in her or his own marriage. A good marriage is an important prerequisite for bringing children into a family, but in many situations there are not two parents to care for the child.

Box 6-1.

Ten Ridiculous Ideas That Will Make You a Parent

1. You can count on your partner to use birth control.
2. Men have stronger sex drives than women do.
3. Men need to have sex with different women to learn to be better lovers.
4. If a woman uses birth control, then she has probably been sleeping around.
5. A woman would do anything to keep from getting pregnant.
6. It is easy for a woman to get on the pill.
7. If a man hasn't "gone all the way" by the time he's 16, then something is wrong with him.
8. Condoms are not cool.
9. When a woman says "no," she really just wants to be talked into it.
10. I could never talk to my partner about birth control.

Source: Adapted with permission from the brochure "Ten Ridiculous Ideas That Will Make a Father Out of You,"

© 1984, Planned Parenthood of Central Oklahoma, 619 N.W. 23rd Street, Oklahoma City, OK 73103.

Teen Pregnancy

Teen pregnancy is an extreme example of losing control of one's life. The United States leads the world in rates of teenage pregnancy and abortion. Adolescent pregnancy in this country can be described as an epidemic: the rate is twice that of France, England, and Canada; three times that of Sweden; and seven times that of the Netherlands.

There are a multitude of negative consequences associated with adolescent pregnancy and motherhood. Though it is true that many young mothers may raise their children successfully, the problems "children having children" encounter can be overwhelming. The father usually disappears from the picture, and the young mother ends up rearing the child alone. This often places an extra burden on the grandparents, who may not be overjoyed to be "parents" again. And although the young mother needs an education to support herself and her child, she may find it difficult to continue in school. Young mothers often experience serious financial problems, inadequate housing, lack of transportation, loneliness, poor nutrition, physical health problems, and a cluster of other stressors that foster a situation in which child neglect and abuse are common.

Single Parenthood

Nearly one in three American families is headed by a single parent. This number has increased dramatically over the past 30 years. In 1970, 11 percent of families were single-parent families; in 1980 the figure had increased to 20 percent; by the mid-1990s it was 31 percent.

Many single parents in this country are doing a good job parenting. They demonstrate affection and concern for their children and work hard to provide stability and educational opportunities in a wholesome environment. In many cases a healthy single-parent family is better than couples where one parent, for example, is alcoholic or has been physically abusive to the other. Growing up in a family torn by abuse of any kind is not a healthy environment for children.

When a person leaves a bad marriage or relationship and begins constructing a new life as a single parent, she or he is likely to face many new challenges:

- *A high level of stress:* simply too many things to worry about and not enough time to accomplish everything that needs to be done.

- *Money problems:* often made more difficult by lack of child support from the other parent.

- *Loneliness and a sense of isolation:* limited energy for developing new friendships after taking care of the kids and working long hours to support them.

- *Continuing battles with ex-partners:* over money issues, how the children should be raised, and how often the noncustodial parent gets to see the children.

Preparation for parenthood and an understanding of the dynamics of family living can help people avoid many problems before they arise. An ounce of prevention clearly is worth a pound of cure. By learning about marriage and family relationships ahead of time, by preparing for the future rather than being swept into it without control, young people can live safer, healthier, and happier lives.

The best preparation for parenthood is to learn about healthy intimate relationships: to learn how to find a good partner, how to develop a successful relationship, and how to enjoy the benefits of that relationship for a long time into the future. It is far better to put a fence at an overlook so people don't fall over the edge, than to have ambulances stationed at the base of the cliff to treat the injured who have fallen off the cliff.

Delaying Parenthood

What are the advantages of delaying parenthood? Let's list a few of the benefits of waiting to have children until you are married and are more secure emotionally and financially.

- *Career advantages:* time to get a good education and get established in a good job or profession, instead of struggling to care for children and scrape together a living from a low-paying and low-status job.

- *Financial advantages:* more money to pay for your education; extra money to buy things you want (new car, large television), a greater likelihood of getting a well-paying job.

- *Maturity advantages:* experience and wisdom about life, maturity makes you a more secure and loving spouse and a calmer and wiser parent; your children will benefit from having more capable and confident parents.

You can be a good parent if for some reason you have children at a young age. But it sure is a lot easier if you become parents when you're more established in your career, when you have a reasonable amount of money coming in, when you feel relatively mature and capable, and when you feel good about your marriage and confident that it has staying power. We all need stability. We all need people we can count on and an environment that is not going to come crashing down around us with little warning.

How Children Change Your Life

Becoming a parent happens overnight, and it changes your life. Forever. Are we exaggerating? No, we are not. Listen to this young father, who expresses the feelings of millions of parents:

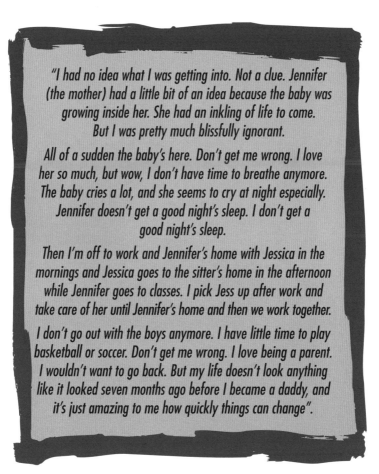

"I had no idea what I was getting into. Not a clue. Jennifer (the mother) had a little bit of an idea because the baby was growing inside her. She had an inkling of life to come. But I was pretty much blissfully ignorant.

All of a sudden the baby's here. Don't get me wrong. I love her so much, but wow, I don't have time to breathe anymore. The baby cries a lot, and she seems to cry at night especially. Jennifer doesn't get a good night's sleep. I don't get a good night's sleep.

Then I'm off to work and Jennifer's home with Jessica in the mornings and Jessica goes to the sitter's home in the afternoon while Jennifer goes to classes. I pick Jess up after work and take care of her until Jennifer's home and then we work together.

I don't go out with the boys anymore. I have little time to play basketball or soccer. Don't get me wrong. I love being a parent. I wouldn't want to go back. But my life doesn't look anything like it looked seven months ago before I became a daddy, and it's just amazing to me how quickly things can change".

Children Impact Your Life Directly

What impact does parenthood have on you as an individual? It affects every aspect of your life. Your time is not your own anymore. Your life revolves around your baby; your life doesn't revolve around you. As one young woman put it, "I don't feel like a human being anymore. I feel like a body and soul invented to serve this little baby."

The time you invest in your newly arrived baby affects how you spend time in all other aspects of your life. Every one of your old satisfactions and priorities are affected, often in ways you are not happy about. You have less time to focus on your education, less time for your job or career, less time for leisure activities, less time for friends, and less time for extended-family members.

AWARE item 2.
Having children will dramatically change your life. (True)

Impact on Your Couple Relationship

Perhaps the most potentially dramatic change that accompanies parenthood is its impact on your relationship with your partner. You have less time for each other. Your focus can no longer be only your own desires as an individual and your need to be with your partner. Now you have to attend to your baby's needs, whether you're happy or sad, whether you're energetic or exhausted, whether you would rather sleep than be up with a baby.

Everybody is in line for your time and money. What tends to happen is that you neglect your own personal needs to some degree. You stop exercising and going out with friends and never seem to get time to read or relax. You are spending less time with each other as a couple and this can create problems for a marriage.

Couples simply cannot afford to forget about their marriage when babies arrive. Many people have found themselves in the sad situation of making the baby happy, making the boss and the bill collectors and everybody else happy, but ending up unhappy personally because they have no time for themselves. People can end up unhappy in their marriage because they forgot to courageously defend their time together as a loving couple.

Why does love go when it disappears from a marriage? It usually disappears because we put our focus and interest on other things. But we simply cannot afford to let this happen, because a happy marriage is the foundation for a strong family.

AWARE item 3.
Having children can have a negative effect on a couple's marriage. (True)

Parenthood: The 24-Hour Job

In any other job are you on call 24 hours a day, seven days a week, 365 days a year, year after year after year? How many jobs do you *never ever* get to retire from? As one 50-year-old man, a father himself, notes:

> "To my mother, I'm still a kid. Maybe a big kid, but still a kid. She still worries about me and wonders what I'm doing. And she feels responsible for the grandkids in many ways. She feels directly connected to them, and wants to make sure, in any way she can, that they have a good life.
>
> She's still my mother, even though she's 80 years old. I'm still her child, even though I'm 50 now. I'm an adult child, to be precise, but I'm still a child. Being a mother has been, literally, a lifelong responsibility for my mother."

"Child-rearing is the only task in the world where your goal is to make your own job obsolete".

--ANONYMOUS

Stresses and Rewards

Despite its many satisfactions, parenthood is clearly stressful. Many of the stresses stem from the fact that the job goes on and on. Parenthood demands a great deal from people, and its rewards are infrequent. First of all, you don't get paid for being a parent. Second, you rarely get thanked for being a parent. On occasion, small children express their appreciation and affection for their parents with a kiss or a hug—they can be especially endearing in this way. But when children get older, especially in the adolescent and young-adult years, many draw away from their parents for at least a few years. During this so-called launching phase, parents who have invested so much in their children's development can feel sorely neglected: "I don't know what's wrong with my daughter," they mutter. "I haven't gotten a letter or a phone call for six weeks!"

Parent: "We haven't heard from you for six weeks. And you never sent a thank-you card to your Aunt Sadie for your graduation present, either."

Young-Adult Child: "I'm so busy now I just never got it done."

This interchange reflects a painful situation for parents that can lead to loneliness and feelings of being abandoned by their young-adult child. But to the launching-phase child, the parent's comments prove once again that parents can be controlling. This all-too-common dynamic leads many parents to conclude that most children do not appreciate the sacrifices their parents make for them. But in defense of the younger generation, how can children have any idea what parents go through until they experience parenthood themselves? Describing parenthood is even more difficult than describing your first kiss. You have to be there to really understand.

Although parents may want to receive praise for their efforts or hugs and kisses from their kids, it just isn't likely to happen. The rewards of parenthood are many, but traditional measures of reward tend to be few. Parents aren't rewarded financially for doing the right thing, day after day. The rewards of parenting are mostly internal: the joy of watching a child grow, watching a child's amazing reactions, the closeness of a good marriage in which both partners work together to raise their youngsters, the satisfaction one feels from a job well done.

In reality, however, we will never be able to repay our parents for all they have done for us. For grandparents this is proof positive that they succeeded in their task of raising responsible human beings. We benefit from our parents' sacrifices, and when you become parents yourselves, you will sacrifice for your own children. All in all, it works out to be a fair system down through the generations. You demonstrate your appreciation by passing your love onto your children.

AWARE item 4.
Taking care of children can be stressful with little reward. (True)

STRESS

Courses in Parenthood

Parents have the most important and challenging job in the world, yet as a society we require no training for that job. But the child and society suffer when someone fails in the job of parenting. We believe that courses in marriage and family relationships can help people learn how to become better parents. But parenting is not just about facts, but about having a plan and learning by doing. Experiential methods of teaching, in which students learn not only by listening but also by doing, are clearly more effective.

One of the arguments against including mandatory classes in marriage and parenting in the school curriculum is that these things are all common sense. If all this comes naturally, however, why is it that at least half of all those who marry today will likely divorce? Why is the rate of marital unhappiness so high? Why is spouse abuse so common? Why are so many children abused or not understood?

The fact is, good marriages and good parent-child relationships don't happen naturally. We are not born with an understanding of nuclear physics. By the same token, we need to learn how to love and care for each other. Families are the first place we start learning about love and caring. Schools can also play an important role in our knowledge of good parenting.

AWARE item 5.
Raising children is a natural activity that requires little training. (False)

Parenthood Is Forever

It's common in our society to hear about the term *ex-spouse*. Divorce is epidemic, and ex-spouses abound. But we don't have any mechanism for becoming an *ex-parent*, nor any terminology to describe such a situation. You can divorce your partner, but you cannot divorce your child. Though it is true that you can relinquish your child for adoption, the fact is you still remain that child's birth mother or birth father. Parenthood is, in essence, forever.

When married couples break up, one parent usually has more responsibility for the day-to-day care of the children than the other parent. A small percentage of couples share child care almost equally after divorce, but in most situations one person does the majority of the day-to-day child-rearing—and most of the time that person is the mother. This does not mean, though, that fathers do not have any responsibility for children after a marriage ends.

Importance of Fathers

Fathers can be very important in their children's development. Fathers can:

- Care for their child(ren) on a regular basis, doing the same things that mothers do—feeding, sheltering, clothing, and teaching them about life. This gives the mother a break from her child-care responsibilities, lessens the stress in her life, and is likely to make her happier and more pleasant when she is with the children.

- Pay his fair share of money for the children's day-to-day care and educational needs. He was just as responsible for bringing the children into the world as their mother was.

- Play an important role as a positive adult male figure in their life, showing them what good men do and feel.

- Treat their mother with respect and support her as a parent. This doesn't have to be all that hard to do. On the job or at school we work or co-exist year after year with people who we don't love and many who we don't even like. We still are quite capable of getting along with them and getting the job done.

Sometimes, of course, the roles are reversed after divorce. Sometimes the father has custody of the children and the mother is the non-custodial parent. The father's responsibilities for his children in this situation are very similar to a mother's responsibilities as a single parent: to provide direct care, education, and financial support for the children. Hopefully, he receives a fair measure of the same types of support from the non-custodial mother.

Sharing Parenting as a Couple

The responsibilities of being a parent are too great and the joys too significant to all fall on the shoulders of one person. This is the basic argument today for getting fathers significantly involved in the day-to-day care of their children. Fortunately, most fathers are perfectly capable of being good parents and can easily understand how important it is, to the children and to themselves as fathers, to be an active participant in the family.

In the so-called **traditional family** in which mother stayed home with the kids and father went off to work outside the home, it was somewhat reasonable for women to do most of the child care and housework in the family. But today, with the majority of mothers working outside the home as well as inside the home, it is only fair that fathers carry their share of the childrearing and household responsibilities. Otherwise, you end up with exhausted and irritable mothers, and that makes for an unhappy home for everyone.

Though many women have been arguing over the past 30 years that men should become more involved with children, in the average American family the mother has more responsibility for the children than the father.

AWARE item 6.
Most couples equally share in parenting responsibilities. (False)

Parenting by Fathers

Why do men do less parenting than mothers? Men are not socialized as children to nurture, but instead are socialized to compete. While little girls are playing house today, little boys are playing roughhouse: wrestling, football, baseball, and so forth. This leads to little interest and little skill later on as husbands in the area of domestic responsibility.

Some mothers find it difficult to give up their power in the home and let fathers become more involved with the children and doing housework. "He wouldn't do a good job, anyway." This gives the mother a rationalization for not being more career oriented outside the home.

Some men do not value doing parenting because it requires doing repetitive tasks. For example:

A husband, a lawyer who loved statistics, volunteered to stay home with the children for a day because the normal daycare provider was ill. When his wife returned he handed her the following report, only partially tongue-in-cheek: dried tears, nine times; tied shoes, four times; cleaned up spills, five times; changed diapers, eight times; fixed meals, three times; broke up fights, ten times; number of times I wanted to do this again, zero.

But parenting by fathers is good for everyone in the family. It is good for mothers. The day-in-day-out burden is lessened, making her feel less pressured. She can be a better mother and better wife because of this. Also, a father caring for the children and doing housework is an indication of the respect he has for what his wife does in life, and the love he has for her as a person. It takes both a man and a woman to create a child, and both are responsible for the care of that child.

It is good for the children. They benefit from two good parents, instead of one. They get to see that adults do things differently and that's okay. And, that males are capable of being kind and nurturing.

It is also good for fathers. Raising children is of critical importance in our society. Fathers should have a chance to contribute their skills in the task of guiding the next generation to inhabit Mother Earth. And besides being important, living with children is just plain fun. Kids are fascinating and lively. They help keep us young. Dads deserve this opportunity.

AWARE item 7.
Most fathers are actively involved in their children's lives. (False)

Creating a Parenting Team

Each couple has to develop an approach to parenthood that works for them, both as individuals and as a parenting team. This is not easy to do. Now we all know that developing any kind of team effort takes a lot of time, discussion, and practice. And this is surely the case when it comes to a couple needing to create a successful parenting team.

The partners probably come from families-of-origin in which parenting styles differed, and this makes discussion of parenting plans essential if the couple is to come to some kind of agreement. The mother's parents may have been easy-going and warm. The father's parents may have been mixed: an emotionally distant father and a nervous mother. Or, the mother's parents might have been very traditional, with Dad going off to work and Mom staying home with the children.

The more different the family-of-origin of the parents, the more likely the couple looks at parenting from different perspectives. It is almost inevitable that they are going to disagree on many issues as parents. He may want her to stay home while the children are young; she may find that impossible, given her career ambitions. She may want him very involved with the day-to-day care of the kids, he may want to spend time playing sports.

Discipline is an especially difficult area for parents, and spouses are most likely to have different views on the best ways to discipline a child. Commonly, fathers tend to be more punitive than mothers, but many mothers have to be both loving and handle discipline if the father is not available.

AWARE item 8.
Most couples agree on how best to discipline their children. (False)

It is important that the couple work together to create a parenting style with which both parents are happy and comfortable. If the mother and father are not working together as a successful parent team, children will learn to manipulate and play mother off against father to get what they want.

Finances As a Source of Conflict

One of the big surprises for most parents is how much it financially costs to raise children. Raising children is a very expensive venture, no matter what a family's income. According to recent U.S. government figures:, the cost varies by income level.

- **Lower-income families** (earning less than $29,900 a year) who raise a child from birth to age 17 spend on average $86,100.

- **Middle-income families** (earning $29,900 to $48,300 a year) who raise a child from birth to age 17 spend on average $120,150.

- **Upper-income families** (earning more than $48,300 a year) raising a child from birth to age 17 spend on average $168,480.

Remember, these figures just get your child through high school. Then you need to figure out how to pay for college, which can cost from $15,000-$50,000 per year of college. See Table 6-1 for details on how much one child costs to raise in a two-parent, middle-income family.

Table 6-1.

How Much Two Parents Spend on One Child In Middle-Income Families

AGE OF CHILD	TOTAL	HOUSING	FOOD	TRANSPORTATION	CLOTHING	HEALTH CARE	EDUCATION CHILD CARE AND OTHER
0-2	$ 6,140	$ 2,330	$ 830	$ 990	$ 400	$ 290	$ 1,300
3-5	6,540	2,270	960	1,050	440	280	1,540
6-8	6,500	2,280	1,220	1,130	470	290	1,110
9-11	6,330	2,150	1,370	1,060	480	300	970
12-14	7,050	2,090	1,450	1,370	790	310	1,040
15-17	7,490	2,060	1,620	1,630	750	320	1,110
TOTAL	$120,150	$39,540	$22,350	$21,690	$9,990	$5,370	$21,210

Source: "Expenditures on a Child by Two-Parent Families" by M. Lino, 1991, Family Economics Review, 4(1), p. 32.
U.S. Department of Agriculture.

How Important Are Parents?

In our society everyone seems to know how important parents are for children. For example, we enjoy asking our students in parenting classes to think about the absolute worst thing you ever did when you were growing up. We say: "Okay, now think carefully. Who was responsible for this silly or stupid act? Who was to blame for it? Your parents or you?" After the laughter dies down, most agree that they chose to do this behavior all by themselves.

It's undoubtedly true that parents have a great deal of influence on their children, modeling good and bad behaviors. But young people learn, beginning at least in early adolescence, to make their own decisions in life. Individuals must be responsible for their own behavior.

Parents are influential in the lives of their children, but children influence the lives of their parents also. For example, if a child is acting out (whether it be getting poor grades in school or having trouble with the law), that behavior will likely cause stress and strain on the parents' relationship. On the other hand, conflict in the parents' marriage can lead some children to act out. This is an example of the concept of circular causality: when two factors are closely related (in this case, marital conflict and the child's behavior), it may not be clear which behavior caused the other. Rather, each seems to have an impact on the other.

It's important to recognize how hard it can be to find the root cause of difficult family problems. Did conflict in the parents' marriage make the child so upset that he or she decided to act out? Or did the child's unruly behavior cause disagreement and conflict between the parents? Or was the concept of circular causality in operation? Did each of these factors influence the other?

Often both parents and children effect each other. For that reason, it is important not to get caught in the "blame game." Blame-game players believe that pointing the finger at somebody else will somehow solve the problem. Remember, when you point a finger to blame another person, three other fingers are pointing back at you.

AWARE item 10.
Marital conflict can have a negative effect on children. (True)

Satisfactions of Parenting

Raising healthy and well-adjusted children can be a source of great joy and accomplishment for parents. Though parenting is challenging, it is also very satisfying for many parents. Researchers surveyed more than 700 parents and recorded the satisfactions they reported. The information they collected appears in Table 6-2.

Table 6-2.

Common Satisfactions of Parenthood

Specific Satisfaction	Percent Recording the Response
Watching children grow and develop	74
Love for children	65
Pride in children's achievement	62
Sharing	54
A growth experience	45
Passing on values	44
Fun to do things with	43
General enjoyment	41
Feeling of being part of a family	40
Self-fulfillment	39
Feel needed	39
Enjoying physical contact	37
Feeling closer to spouse	36
A purpose for living	32
Enjoying the simple aspects of life	31
Companionship	27

Source: "Parent Satisfactions: Implications for Strengthening Families" (p. 147) by W. H. Meredith, N. Stinnett, and B. F. Cacioppo. In Family Strengths 6: Enhancement of Interaction, edited by R. Williams. H. Lingren, G. Rowe, S.Van Zandt, P. Lee, and N. Stinnett, 1985, Lincoln, NE; Department of Human Development and the Family, Center for Family Strengths, University of Nebraska. Copyright 1985 by Center for Family Strengths. Reprinted by Permission.

This father explains the pleasures of parenting very well:

"I can't imagine a life without my children," said Terry, a 45-year-old businessman from Detroit. "Sure, I get mad at them. They bug me, and I yell at them once in a while. But I love them so much, and their journey through life is so much fun to watch. I keep wondering: 'What's the next chapter of the story going to be? What are they going to do next? What will they all become?'" "I suppose I could have concentrated on my career more if I hadn't had children, but love has always counted far more to me than money."

Are You Ready to Be a Parent?

Couples need to talk with each other honestly about parenthood. If one partner really wants children and the other doesn't know for sure, it's important to discuss this before, rather than after, marriage. Couples cannot reach some kind of magical agreement without talking. Some couples fall into parenthood by accident, which can be problematic.

As couples discuss parenthood together, they need to try to understand why one partner feels the way he or she does. They should think about whether they plan to have children and if so, when. The following list provides some guidelines to help couples decide when they might be ready for parenthood:

1. *You have a happy and stable marriage.* Don't jump into parenthood right away. Give your marriage some time to develop. Get used to living with each other and make sure you genuinely enjoy the life of a married couple. If you have any concerns about your marriage, it's best to postpone children until you've worked out your problems. Children will not make things better. Instead, they can make them even worse.

2. *Your finances are adequate.* If you have debts, try to pay off as many of them as possible before having children. Also, try to save some money. Establish an emergency fund —money to support the family for several months if you and/or your partner were to lose your job. Make sure you know how to budget money. Then take your budget for two and adjust it to accommodate a third member of the family.

3. *You do not feel pressured into having a child.* Do not become parents to make somebody else happy. Become parents because you genuinely want to become parents. The decision is yours as a couple.

4. *You have both agreed that this is the time to have a child.* Deciding "when" is the next challenge. You can't predict with certainty when you'll become pregnant, and adoption is even more difficult to plan. Look carefully at what is happening in your lives in the near future and beyond, and talk about better and worse times to have a child.

5. *You are ready for a major change in your personal life and marriage.* Parenthood will change your life forever. There's no going back. Many of the changes will be joyful, but even good things in life can cause stress. Discuss honestly with your partner the concerns you have and come to an agreement about how to deal with the changes parenthood will bring.

Marriage As the Foundation for Family

Once again, it's important to remember that a strong marriage is the foundation for a strong family. Children need parents who love them. They also need parents who love each other. As parents, one of the greatest gifts we can give our children is to love each other. Don't let the stresses of parenthood and life in general overwhelm your marriage. Make time for your couple relationship. Many people have made the mistake of being good as parents and good as employees, but bad as partners—and their partnership ended in divorce.

⁓

You might find it informative now to go back and respond again to the AWARE Scale, "Children and Parenting," at the beginning of this chapter. See what you've learned.

7 Communication Skills

> **"** We hear only half of what is said to us, understand only half of that, believe only half of that and remember only half of that. **"**
>
> MIGNON MCLAUGHLIN, JOURNALIST

How is Your Communication?

Circle True or False

1 Men and women have different styles of communicating.　　T or F

2 Nonverbal communication often reveals true feelings that verbal communication may conceal.　　T or F

3 Communication is a skill that can be learned and improved.　　T or F

4 Assertiveness is valuable because it lets others know what you want and need.　　T or F

5 Partners often know what the other partner thinks and feels without being told.　　T or F

6 A couple's style of communicating during dating will carry over into marriage.　　T or F

7 Couples' communication often improves after marriage.　　T or F

8 Couples often avoid talking about topics that may cause arguments or disagreements.　　T or F

9 Most couples find it easy to talk about their relationship.　　T or F

10 It is possible to not communicate.　　T or F

Please complete the QUIZ before reading the chapter.

Communication - An Essential Skill

Communication is at the heart of intimate relationships. It is the foundation on which all else is built. Communication is the way humans create and share meaning, both verbally and nonverbally. The ability to communicate is one of a handful of essential skills individuals must master if they are to enjoy close relationships. In fact, the ability and the willingness to communicate have been found to be among the most important factors in maintaining a satisfying relationship.

Communication difficulties often arise when individuals have divergent communication styles. The two most significant sources of communication-style differences are gender and culture.

Gender Differences in Communication Style

Common gender-related differences in communication often cause conflict between men and women. It sometimes seems as if there are two distinct styles of communication: a masculine style and a feminine style. A better understanding by men and women of the differences between the two styles can reduce some of the friction between the genders.

Competition vs. Connection

Men often use conversation in a competitive way, perhaps in an attempt to establish dominance in a relationship. Women tend to use conversation in a connective way, hoping to establish friendship. Females tend to use good listening behaviors (such as eye contact, frequent nodding, focused attention, and relevant questions). Females tend to speak as a way to connect with people and ideas. Men on the other hand, focus less on listening and more on responding. Men are more likely than women to interrupt while another person is speaking. They often continue with another activity instead of giving the speaker undivided attention. Males also tend to talk more but to disclose less personal information about themselves.

Men are generally socialized to be competitive. Their world is hierarchical—emphasizing rank, position, and social class—and each encounter with another person is seen as a challenge to their status. When an interaction is over, men often evaluate themselves as one-up or one-down. Male conversations are almost symbolic struggles in which the competitor tries to gain the upper hand, protect himself from threatening moves, and not allow himself to be pushed around. Because feelings can be falsely interpreted as signs of weakness, men are more uncomfortable talking about feelings than women are.

Women tend to approach the world not as competing, independent individuals, but as people intimately interconnected with one another. Women tend to "network"; men tend to "compete." If you want to learn more about this issue, we recommend Deborah Tannen's book, *You Just Don't Understand: Women and Men in Conversation* (1990). Tannen states that for women, conversations are "negotiations for closeness in which people try to seek and give confirmation and support, and to reach consensus." Women tend to seek out a community and to work to preserve intimacy and avoid isolation. Although women are also concerned with achieving status and avoiding failure, these are not their major focuses in life.

Tannen explains women's "nagging" as a different approach to living. Women are inclined to do what people ask them to do. Men, on the other hand, tend to resist even the slightest hint that someone else—especially a woman—has the authority to tell them what to do. Women tend to repeat their requests of men—to "nag"—because they assume men think the same as women. "He would, of course, want to do what I'm asking if he only understood what I want."

AWARE item 1.
Men and women have different styles of communicating. (True)

Seeking Solutions vs. Sharing Feelings

Men also tend to focus on solutions to problems, whereas women focus on sharing what they are feeling about problems. Because of this difference in focus, men often feel that women "only talk" about problems, and women often feel frustrated and misunderstood.

Who is at fault? Neither. Both are simply reflecting masculine and feminine gender roles in their conversational styles. Tannen is careful to point out that women also value freedom and independence but tend to emphasize **interdependence** and connection more. Similarly, men are more socialized to see independence as most important.

Tannen argues that both sexes could learn from one another. Women could learn to accept some conflict and difference without considering it a threat to intimacy. Men could learn from women that interdependence is not a threat to personal freedom. Tannen believes the "best" style of communication is a flexible one—a delicate balance between independence and connectedness.

In summary, men tend to communicate in a world where they are trying to establish a position of power. Women traditionally have not been invited to run with the "big dogs." They have not been allowed, historically, into the corporate boardrooms and government cabinet meetings where the "big decisions" are made. Instead of playing dominance games, women developed a culture of communication based on connection. Today, the picture has changed to a certain degree. A woman has been chosen Secretary of State to help guide our nation's foreign policy, and countless men are at home taking care of their babies.

Cultural Differences in Communication Style

The use and interpretation of both verbal and nonverbal communication vary widely from culture to culture. In England, for example, gestures are considered to be bold and undesirable additions to the communication process. But in Italy, France, and the Polynesian islands of the southwest Pacific, gesturing is common and accepted.

Cultural differences can affect not only how well a message is understood but also the way in which the messenger is perceived as an individual. A student from India related the following incident, which occurred when he first arrived in the United States. The student was fairly fluent in English, but he was totally unfamiliar with American customs. One day he was walking down the street with a fellow student with whom he had become good friends. Without giving it much thought, he reached toward his friend and took his hand as they continued walking. Having assumed his Indian friend was heterosexual, the American student was somewhat startled and asked his friend why he wanted to hold hands. The Indian student became confused and said it was customary in India for two close friends to hold hands to show their friendship.

Clearly, actions may be interpreted quite differently in different cultures. The nature and scope of our nonverbal behavior is largely determined by our cultural heritage. For example, the different ways in which men react to beautiful women around the world have been documented. The American male lifts his eyebrows, the Italian presses his forefinger into his cheek and rotates it, the Greek strokes his cheek, the Brazilian puts an imaginary telescope to his eye, the Frenchman kisses his fingertips, and the Egyptian grasps his beard.

Westerners consider direct eye contact important—a sign of friendship, honesty, and strength. But many cultures see it as a personal affront. In Japan, for example, when shaking hands, bowing, and especially when talking, it is important to glance only occasionally into the other person's face. Instead, individuals focus their gaze on fingertips, desk tops, and carpets. In the words of one American electronics representative, "Always keep your shoes shined in Tokyo. You can bet a lot of Japanese you meet will have their eyes on them."

In most Latin countries, from Venezuela to Italy, the abrazo (hug) is as common as a handshake. Men hug men, women hug women,

men hug women. In Slavic countries, this greeting is better described as a bear hug. In France, the double cheek-to-cheek greeting is common among both men and women. But the Japanese are averse to casual touching, preferring a traditional bow from the waist. Americans may feel uncomfortable with bowing, but to the Japanese, it means, "I respect your experience and wisdom."

Verbal vs. Nonverbal Communication

In communicating with other people, it is important to pay close attention to nonverbal messages. In fact, some researchers estimate that nearly 65 percent of all face-to-face communication is nonverbal. It is ironic, then, how carefully we select our words, when they comprise only 35 percent of the message we communicate, and how little attention we sometimes pay to the nonverbal message we are also conveying.

Verbal communication includes both spoken and written words. Spoken communication has various nonverbal aspects to it: tone of voice, volume, pitch, speed, and rhythm. Written communication also has nonverbal aspects: style of writing (handwritten, printed, typed, sloppy, neat) and the medium (personal stationery, a card, a napkin).

Nonverbal communication takes a wide variety of other forms. It includes facial expressions, eye contact, gestures, and other body movements, spatial behavior (e.g., how close a person stands or sits to another), body contact, nonverbal vocalizations (e.g., sighs, grunts), and posture. Nonverbal communication is just as difficult to interpret as verbal communication. Is that yawn boredom, or is it a simple reflexive action caused by inactivity or boredom.

One component of communication that has a central influence on the accurate transmission and interpretation of nonverbal messages is the relationship context. For example, if you see two people hugging at the airport, you assume they have a close relationship. In other words, we make guesses about a relationship based on nonverbal behavior and the context in which we observe that behavior.

Researchers have found that a couple's nonverbal communication is related to the type of overall relationship they have. Couples who showed little disagreement during topical discussions tended to sit more closely together, touch each other more frequently, and establish a greater amount of eye contact than couples who disagreed a great deal during those discussions. Moreover, husbands and wives who complained quite a bit about their relationship sat farther apart, established minimal eye contact, and talked more than any other type of couple in the study. Couples who voiced few complaints showed the greatest amount of nonverbal affection and caring, including touching one another, assuming open-arm and leg postures, and maintaining eye contact.

Content vs. Feelings

Verbal communication, more often than not, focuses on content—on information the speaker wants to convey. It is widely believed by communication researchers that nonverbal communication more often focuses on feelings: how the individual feels about what is happening. Because of this, we can often learn a lot more about what is going on in a relationship by what we see and sense than by what we hear. Understanding nonverbal communication is the intuitive process. An experienced counselor describes this type of intuition this way:

> "I'll be sitting with a client and they'll be insisting that what somebody did was not in the least bit hurtful to them. They'll be insisting that it didn't cause them any stress. But their body will be telling me something else. They will be speaking rapidly, almost breathlessly, about the incident. They will be blinking their eyes over and over again. Their eyes will be wide open and they'll have a look on their face of total awareness and emotional arousal. They might have reddish splotches on their neck. Just thinking back on the incident with the other person gets them all wired. And you know, with some people who are under stress, they start to smell different. I know that sounds crazy, but I can feel stress in my clients!"

This counselor knows intuitively what is going on inside the client, even though the client verbally denies being upset.

AWARE item 2.
Nonverbal communication often reveals true feelings that verbal communication may conceal. (True)

Mixed Messages

The client communication the counselor just described is also a good example of a mixed message. People often send messages in which the verbal and the nonverbal components do not agree. The listener hears one thing but simultaneously feels something else. When the verbal and the nonverbal parts of a message conflict, we tend to rely more on the nonverbal information because we sense that it is more accurate than what is being said.

We all send mixed messages every day for a variety of reasons, but unwillingness to communicate directly and honestly is often the reason. Mixed messages can become a barrier to real understanding. Communication directly minimizes misunderstanding and confusion. Besides, it is almost impossible to hide our true feelings long. A person's true feelings usually escape, one way or another.

Good Communication—A Team Effort

Good communication is a team effort because it takes a good speaker and a good listener. We have to work together to get the message across. The ability to communicate does not come naturally. We learn it from one another. From people who are good communicators, we learn skillful and effective communication. From people who are bad communicators, we may pick up ineffective communication habits.

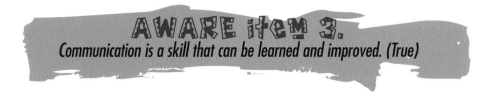

AWARE item 3.
Communication is a skill that can be learned and improved. (True)

"It takes two to speak the truth...one to speak and another to hear".
— HENRY DAVID THOREAU, PHILOSOPHER

Assertiveness & Active Listening

Assertiveness *is a person's ability to express their feelings and ask for what they would like.* When two people know what the other wants—when they both know they have been heard and understood—intimacy is increased. Assertiveness also helps people feel good about themselves and increases the likelihood that they will achieve their personal goals.

Here are two examples of assertive statements:

I enjoy spending time with you, but I also want to spend more time with my friends. I would like us to find some time to talk about this.

I want to go to the beach next winter, but I know you like to go skiing.

AWARE item 4.
Assertiveness is valuable because it lets others know what you want and need. (True)

Active Listening

Good communication depends on people listening carefully to each other. **Active listening** *involves listening attentively without interrupting and then restating what was heard.* The active listening process lets the speaker know whether the message sent was clearly understood because the listener restates what he or she heard. Here are two examples:

> "I heard you say that you enjoy the time we spend together, but that you need more time to be with your friends. You want to plan a time to talk about this."

> "If I understood what you said, you want to go to the beach next winter. But you think I would probably rather go skiing. Is that correct?"

Many arguments between loved ones begin because they simply do not take the time to listen to one another and to understand what the other is saying. It is important to develop active listening skills so that we accurately hear what others are saying. Although this may sound simple, it is not. If it were the world would not be burdened by so much misunderstanding and conflict.

Couples often mistakenly believe that because they love one another they know every detail of how the other will feel about something. This is fantasy. It is fed by the fear that if we talk deeply about things, we will see how different we really are. However, the fact is that all human beings are unique and therefore different from one another. Even the closest, most loving couples differ on issues. It is important to communicate carefully and explain our beliefs to prevent turmoil.

AWARE item 5.
Partners often know what the other partner thinks and feels without being told. (False)

Value of Assertiveness Versus Avoidance

As we've already discussed in this chapter, **assertiveness** is the ability to express your feelings and ask for what you want. Assertiveness decreases the chances of communication problems, since the message sender clearly states their feelings and wishes, which also increases the probability that they will get what they want. Often times people will indirectly 'hint' at their desires and then are surprised or angry when others do not relate to them accordingly. In other words, being assertive increases the odds that the things you want to happen will happen.

Assertiveness also has another important benefit. There is a positive cycle linking assertiveness and self confidence. In the positive cycle, as a person uses more assertiveness, their level of self confidence increases. As a person's self confidence increases, their willingness and ability to be more assertive increases.

Two other ways that people relate to one another are *avoidance* and *dominance*. **Avoidance** is a person's tendency to minimize issues and their reluctance to deal with issues directly (particularly problematic issues). **Dominance** is defined as others trying to control you and your life. There is a negative cycle linking avoidance and perceived dominance. In this negative cycle, when one person perceives another as dominating, a common reaction is for that person to avoid dealing with issues. As a person uses more avoidance, they will often feel more dominated in their communication with others (see Figure 7-1).

Figure 7-1.

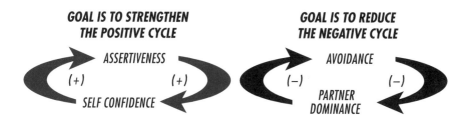

GOAL IS TO STRENGTHEN
THE POSITIVE CYCLE

ASSERTIVENESS
(+)   (+)
SELF CONFIDENCE

GOAL IS TO REDUCE
THE NEGATIVE CYCLE

AVOIDANCE
(−)   (−)
PARTNER
DOMINANCE

A national survey of 2,766 premarital couples who took the PREPARE Inventory found that the more assertive the person, the less they avoided dealing with issues. Also, the more assertive the person, the more they liked the personality of their partner and the more they liked their couple communication and the way they resolved conflict. So assertiveness is a very important relationship skill that people should be encouraged to use with others. Conversely, the more a person avoided communication and dealing with issues, the less assertive they were and the more they disliked their partner.

Communication Barriers in Marriage

People tend to be creatures of habit. We sit in the same seat in a classroom, drive the same route to work, and eat the same food for breakfast—day after day. Couple relationships also become habitual and this can happen all too quickly. While we are dating, we tend to establish communication patterns that will often continue into marriage.

AWARE item 6.

A couple's style of communicating during dating will carry over into marriage. (True)

Communication Patterns Develop Early

The communication patterns you establish in dating carry over into marriage and often become more negative. Communication patterns can be changed, but old habits die slowly. Changing patterns of communication is a difficult challenge that takes the cooperation and creativity of both partners working together.

> *"It took a terrible argument as we were driving home, but we finally started to understand each other," the young husband said.*
>
> *"Yes," his wife added. "We had gotten into a strange pattern. I don't know how it developed. But he would always play the optimist in our marriage, and I would play the pessimist. We didn't know how to really communicate openly and honestly with each other yet—even though we had been married more than seven years."*
>
> *He laughed. "It was crazy sometimes. We would be making a decision about something—about the kids' schooling or money matters or whatever— and Sally would always seem to point out the difficulties and problems. So, to balance things out, I'd always point out the good things, the positive things. I'd even anticipate her negativity and just focus on the positive."*

We tend to think that communication will get better after marriage. Something magical will happen, because we have said our vows and are wearing rings signifying our commitment. Instead, communication problems tend to increase over time. Once we get used to one another, we take off our "good behavior" masks and tend to "get real." Unless we work diligently at practicing good communication patterns, a relationship can easily unravel into more negative communication.

AWARE item 7.
Couples' communication often improves after marriage. (False)

Avoiding Conflict in Communication

One human tendency conspires with all the others to make communication difficult in relationships: our tendency to avoid problems rather than talk about them. We think that if we do not bring up a problem, it will somehow disappear. But a communication problem is like a leaky roof on a house, as time goes by it gets worse, not better.

Avoiding issues does not solve them. Bringing up differences can lead to arguments, it's true. But if we learn and practice the principles of effective communication, we can solve our problems without hurting others. Most of us can learn to communicate effectively, just as we can learn to rollerskate or ride a bicycle. We just need a willingness to learn not to avoid differences but to deal with them directly.

AWARE item 8.

Couples often avoid talking about topics that may cause arguments or disagreements. (True)

Communicating about Communication

We have made it clear that there are major barriers to successful communication between people. We tend to assume we can read each other's mind without talking things out and we avoid discussing problems rather than trying to work them out *together*.

Communication about the quality (good or bad) of a relationship is not always easy, but it is very important if you want to improve the relationship. Talking about how you each communicate will help you learn about ways to improve your communication and increase the closeness you feel toward each other.

AWARE item 9.
Most couples find it easy to talk about their relationship. (False)

Metacommunication, *which means, literally, communication about communication.* We need to be able to sit down and discuss with each other calmly and reasonably our communication processes. We need to develop ground rules and guidelines for discussing problems.

Everything we say or do communicates something to others. We are always communicating. You have probably heard many times that "our actions speak louder than our words"—our nonverbal communication often sends the real message. You may think, for example, that by being quiet you are not communicating. But someone observing you might think that you are upset—so you have communicated something to that person. In fact, it is impossible to not communicate.

AWARE item 10.
It is possible to not communicate. (False)

Now that you have completed this chapter on communication skills, you should go back and respond to the AWARE Quiz on "Communication" once more. Then you can see how you have improved.

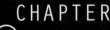

CHAPTER

8 Conflict Resolution Skills

> **Let us never negotiate out of fear, but let us never fear to negotiate.**
>
> JOHN F. KENNEDY

Can You Resolve Conflict?

Circle True or False

1 The more intimate the relationship, the greater the opportunity for conflict.　　　　　T or F

2 People fight mainly over important issues in their relationship.　　　　　T or F

3 People should avoid conflict with each other.　　　　　T or F

4 An argument can often strengthen a relationship.　　　　　T or F

5 To avoid hurting someone's feelings when something is bothering you, it is best to say nothing.　　　　　T or F

6 Problems will disappear over time if they are just left alone.　　　　　T or F

7 When people have conflict, they tend to fight fairly.　　　　　T or F

8 In order to end an argument, it is better to give in.　　　　　T or F

9 Bringing up the past often creates more conflict.　　　　　T or F

10 When there is a problem in a relationship, usually both people are at fault.　　　　　T or F

Please complete the QUIZ before reading the chapter.

Intimacy Breeds Conflict

A paradox of close relationships is that the more intimate two people become, the more chances there are for disagreement and conflict. Arthur Schopenhauer's allegory of the porcupines expresses this concept well:

> A number of porcupines huddled together for warmth on a cold day in winter; but because they began to prick each other with their quills, they were obliged to disperse. However, the cold drove them together again, when just the same thing happened. At last, after many turns of huddling and dispersing, they discovered that they would be best off by remaining at a little distance from each other.

Human beings are very much like porcupines. We are social beings and have a great need to band together for comfort and warmth. The family is our most intimate environment, the one in which we live most closely together. Because of this, we experience conflict in our couple and family relationships more than in any of our other relationships.

To avoid conflict at work and school, we give each other space—both physical space and emotional space. We sometimes call this space "breathing room." What that basically means is that each of us needs the freedom to be ourselves, to make our own decisions, to have our own thoughts and beliefs.

In a family, the stakes are higher than they are at work or school. We depend on others in our family much more than we depend on our more casual acquaintances outside the home. Because we live so close together at home, and because our needs are greater and the stakes are higher among couples and families, conflicts generally heat up quicker and hotter than elsewhere.

AWARE item 1.
The more intimate the relationship, the greater the opportunity for conflict. (True)

Little Things Become Big Irritants

Conflict is an inevitable aspect of all human relationships. In fact, the closer two people become, the more likely they are to experience conflict. As partners and family members we live in such close proximity, it is often seemingly little, unimportant things that upset us in big ways. In the closeness of an intimate relationship, habits or differences become more apparent, and can become annoying. A healthy way to look at this is to realize that personal differences are what make us unique. Learning to enjoy our differences is better than choosing to fight over them.

Think about the last four or five arguments you've had with your loved ones. Chances are that you remember the emotions and the anger of the confrontation, but it's more difficult to remember what the fight was all about.

AWARE item 2.
People fight mainly over important issues in their relationship. (False)

The Hierarchy of Conflict

The hierarchy of conflict model (Figure 8-1) demonstrates how a small issue can potentially turn into a huge issue when it isn't resolved. The three lower levels depict common reasons that people get together: *to chat about daily events, to share ideas, and to express feelings.* These discussions generally occur without stress or tension because there is no need for decision making. The top four levels, however, call for more discussion and decision making. They are, therefore, also more stressful.

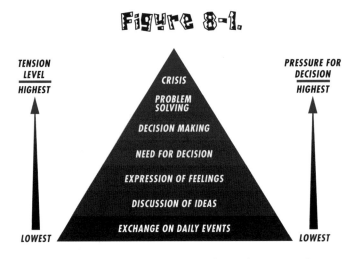

Figure 8-1.

For example, a teenager needs to make a decision about a summer job. She does not want to continue looking for a job because she wants to have some free time during the summer to spend with friends and is planning to go on a camping trip with some of these friends. This turns into a battle with her parents, even though the discussion starts calmly enough at the dinner table one evening:

Father: So, Sarah, how did your day go?
[First level: Exchange on daily events]

Mother: Yes, I'm interested in your job search.
[Second level: Discussion of ideas]

Sarah: Oh, not so good. I went to four places to ask about summer jobs, and they all wanted me to work 40 hours a week. Worse than that, none of them wanted to give me any time off, so I wouldn't be able to go camping in Colorado with Mary Ellen and Ashley. I guess it looks like I won't be working this summer. [Second level: Discussion of ideas]

*Father: I can understand you want to spend time with your friends, but you know, you've got to save some money for college if you're going to go away to school. **[Second level: Discussion of ideas]***

*Sarah: Oh, Dad, I know. But that's a long way off and I'm sick of school right now. **[Third level: Expression of feelings]***

*Mother: I'm sick of a lot of things, but you still need to earn some money for college. **[Third level: Expression of feelings]***

*Sarah: Mother, don't get so mad. You seem to think your life is the hardest life of anybody in the family, I'm sick of going to school, sick of getting up so early in the morning, sick of everything. **[Third level: Expression of feelings]***

Father: Now, look. Both of you calm down. We're going to have to figure this out. There must be some way to balance money and friendship here.
[Fourth level: Need for decision]

Sarah: [Leaving the table to retreat to her bedroom] Money, money, money! That's all you two think about. I can't stand this!
[Third level: Expression of feelings]

Three days later the family is at the dinner table again. For the past two nights they have gone their separate ways, finding excuses not to be around each other at dinnertime. Thursday night, however, they sit down together again.

*Father: Okay, we can't avoid the issue any longer. Let's talk about Sarah's summer job. **[Fourth level: Need for decision]***

Mother: Dad's right, Sarah. You've simply got to get a summer job.
[Fifth level: Decision making]

Sarah: But I can't! I won't get any vacation time, and I won't get to see my friends. It will just be work work work work work again. I won't do it!
[Sixth level: Problem solving]

*Father: What do you mean you won't! If you don't work, you won't be able to save any money for college. **[Sixth level: Problem solving]***

*Mother: And if you don't work, you won't get any allowance from us, so you won't have any money to go camping either. **[Sixth level: Problem solving]***

Sarah: I don't care. I've got some money saved from Grandma.
[Sixth level: Problem solving]

Father: And I won't let you take the car to go camping!
[Sixth level: Problem solving]

*Sarah: Then I'll walk! **[And she does, slamming the front door behind her and precipitating the Seventh level in the hierarchy of conflict: a crisis in the family.]***

This family did just about everything wrong as they stumbled into this conflict with one another. An issue that could have been solved rather easily if the family members had worked together, quickly got out of hand as their emotions took over.

Conflict Is Natural and Should Not Be Avoided

Conflict is natural. It cannot be avoided, and it should not be. Because we are all different, we look at the world from different perspectives. Thus, our views of what is right and wrong and what should be and should not be are often at odds.

AWARE item 3.
People should avoid conflict with each other. (False)

In and of itself, conflict is not dangerous to a relationship. What can be dangerous is our handling of conflict. A relationship can often be strengthened by a constructive discussion, with open communication, without blaming, and without verbal or physical violence. When we get an issue that is bothering us out in the open, we have a genuine opportunity to solve the problem and feel better about one another and our relationship.

AWARE item 4.
An argument can often strengthen a relationship. (True)

Don't Avoid Negative Issues

We often choose to suppress negative feelings to avoid conflict with others. But if negative emotions such as anger and hurt are not resolved, they continue to grow. Or we may suppress our negative feelings about someone so long that we eventually feel nothing— either negative or positive—for that person. We create a devitalized, or burned-out relationship.

Relationships tend to end when people take either of two extreme approaches to conflict resolution: avoidance or overreaction. Partners who avoid discussing conflicts may end up with no feelings for each other, neither hating nor loving one another.

Partners who are overly emotional in their hostilities toward each other, often cannot solve their differences successfully either. In some relationships, one partner may be openly hostile when a conflict arises, yelling and throwing things, and even hitting. The other partner may take a different approach, shutting down emotionally and refusing to enter into the discussion or argument in any way. Neither approach is helpful to resolving issues.

AWARE item 5.
To avoid hurting someone's feelings when something is bothering you, it is best to say nothing. (False)

Tackle Problems Right Away

Human conflicts are like automobiles in many ways. When your car's engine blows up on the freeway, you can't simply walk away and come back in three days and expect it to run. Instead, you've got to get it towed and either fix it yourself or pay someone else to take care of it. Likewise, you can't walk away from a relationship and expect that it will work magically when you return. Problems do not disappear over time.

In fact, relationship problems tend to become bigger if they are not attended to. The argument between mother, father, and teenage daughter over getting a summer job simply got worse after the family members separated from the first round of battle for three days. None of the family members got any better at solving conflicts in the three days because they weren't speaking to one another. A second, even worse explosion was almost inevitable when they got back together.

AWARE item 6.
Problems will disappear over time if they are just left alone. (False)

Anger: Myths and Facts

> *"In all matters of opinion, our adversaries are insane."*
> *— MARK TWAIN, writer and humorist*

Though conflict is inevitable, anger is not. We can learn how to control our anger while at the same time working out conflicts with other people in peaceful, creative ways. Bill Borcherdt notes that, *"Of all human emotions, anger has created the most harm and caused the greatest destruction within individuals, couples, families, and between social groups and nations."*

Anger is truly a double-edged sword: when a person is angry with others, the anger also negatively affects the angry person. As Borcherdt puts it: *"It is impossible to hate, despise, or resent somebody without suffering oneself."* Although anger can sometimes make us feel good, it often can also make us feel guilty and less positive about ourselves.

Anger can produce a temporary feeling of strength and power. It deludes us into thinking that we are doing something constructive about the problems we face, when actually we are only making things worse. Anger lets us substitute feelings of superiority for those of hurt and rejection. It also allows us to think anything we want about others without fear of retaliation.

Four common but false beliefs about anger are that it is externally caused, that it is best to express anger openly and directly, that anger can be a helpful and beneficial emotion, and that if you don't get angry, other people will take advantage of you. Let's look closely at each of these false beliefs.

- *Anger is caused by others.* Many people believe that "somebody else makes you angry or gets you upset," according to Borcherdt. However, our happiness or unhappiness is not externally caused. Anger, like any other human emotion, is self-created, usually when someone else does something we do not like.

- *The best way to deal with anger is to "let it all hang out."* The trouble with this idea is that it may make us feel better for the moment, but it won't help things get any better. Letting it all hang out does not resolve the underlying issues. Also, venting of feelings tends to bring out similar feelings in others, increasing anger in both parties.

- *Anger is a beneficial emotion.* We may find that, in the short run, we get our way more often by getting angry. But in the long run, anger pushes others away. People who are targets of our anger may also try to get even.

- *You're a "wimp" if you don't get angry.* This myth about anger holds that if we don't counterattack every time we are attacked, we are weak, inferior "pansies." But instead of getting angry, we can simply respond directly and rationally. By calmly making statements such as, "I disagree" or "I don't like that," we express how we feel about issues without escalating the conflict.

See Box 8-1 for several other facts and myths about anger.

BOX 8-1.

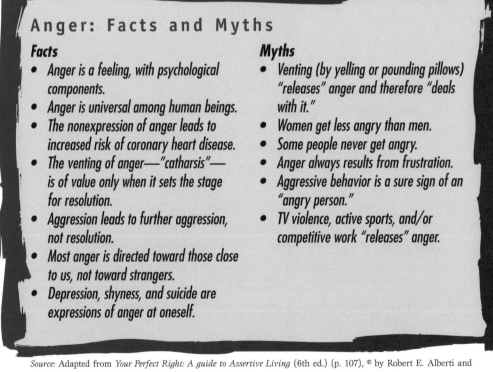

Anger: Facts and Myths

Facts

- Anger is a feeling, with psychological components.
- Anger is universal among human beings.
- The nonexpression of anger leads to increased risk of coronary heart disease.
- The venting of anger—"catharsis"— is of value only when it sets the stage for resolution.
- Aggression leads to further aggression, not resolution.
- Most anger is directed toward those close to us, not toward strangers.
- Depression, shyness, and suicide are expressions of anger at oneself.

Myths

- Venting (by yelling or pounding pillows) "releases" anger and therefore "deals with it."
- Women get less angry than men.
- Some people never get angry.
- Anger always results from frustration.
- Aggressive behavior is a sure sign of an "angry person."
- TV violence, active sports, and/or competitive work "releases" anger.

Source: Adapted from *Your Perfect Right: A guide to Assertive Living* (6th ed.) (p. 107), © by Robert E. Alberti and Michael. L. Emmons, 1990, San Luis Obispo, CA: Impact. Adapted by permission of Impact Publishers, Inc., P.O. Box 1094, San Luis Obispo, CA 94306.

Fighting Fairly: Sixteen Ground Rules

The terms *fight* and *fighting* are commonly used in our society to describe verbal disagreements between people. They are also used to describe boxing matches and other physically violent encounters.

When family therapists talk about rules for fair fighting, they are talking about rules to govern verbal exchanges. Calling verbal conflict a fight is useful. It draws attention to the fact that verbal disagreements are serious business and should be treated with caution and good sense. Tension and anger build up during these exchanges, and verbal conflict can turn into physical conflict.

People should observe certain conventions when arguing with each other, because they will feel safer disagreeing if they know that the situation will not get out of hand. People need to be able to trust each other. We need to know instinctively that others will not leave simply because we disagree with him or her. We will not be taken advantage of if we express our pain and vulnerability. We need to learn how to act in an aboveboard, straightforward, honest manner with each other. This is very difficult, but it is essential in building a good and loving relationship. Unfortunately, when we are in conflict with one another, we tend to fight dirty rather than fairly.

AWARE item 7.
When people have conflict, they tend to fight fairly. (False)

Sixteen ground rules for fair fighting are listed in Box 8-2 and discussed in detail below:

Box 8-2.

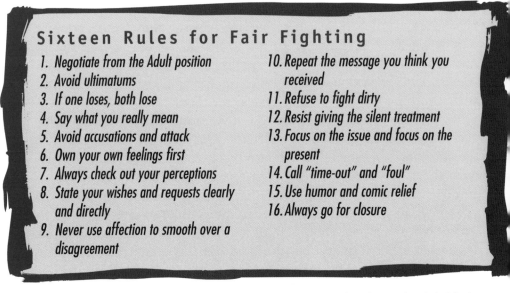

Sixteen Rules for Fair Fighting

1. Negotiate from the Adult position
2. Avoid ultimatums
3. If one loses, both lose
4. Say what you really mean
5. Avoid accusations and attack
6. Own your own feelings first
7. Always check out your perceptions
8. State your wishes and requests clearly and directly
9. Never use affection to smooth over a disagreement
10. Repeat the message you think you received
11. Refuse to fight dirty
12. Resist giving the silent treatment
13. Focus on the issue and focus on the present
14. Call "time-out" and "foul"
15. Use humor and comic relief
16. Always go for closure

Source: Illusion and Disillusion (pp. 170-180) by J. Crosby, 1991, Belmont, CA: Wadsworth. copyright 1991 by J. Crosby, Reprinted by permission of the publisher.

1. Negotiate from the Adult Position. People often replay old "tapes" in their minds. Under stress, people are likely to act as they did when they were children, or as a parent acted toward them. To borrow terminology from transactional analysis, an approach to relationships, when we negotiate from the Child position, we act vulnerable and often feel hurt or threatened.

When we negotiate from the Parent position, we rigidly repeat arguments and views our parents held rather than interacting in new, positive ways. But when we negotiate from the Adult position, we can listen carefully to one another, respond assertively and rationally rather than aggressively and irrationally, and work with the other person to find a solution acceptable to both.

2. Avoid Ultimatums. An ultimatum is a demand: "You do this or else!" It is a hallmark of dirty fighting. Fair fighting emphasizes negotiation and gives each person room to bargain. Ultimatums generally lead to counter-ultimatums, leaving little room for genuine negotiation. An ultimatum puts the receiver in the Child position, with the sender in the Parent position. Neither person gets a chance to negotiate from the Adult position.

3. If One Loses, Both Lose. American society emphasizes competition in the marketplace, but in families competition can be problematic. One partner may be especially good at debating and may "win" most of the arguments. The other person may accuse the partner of using big words or sophisticated logic and is not likely to be happy about the situation.

The better debater may win the argument but lose just as surely as the other does. The relationship has lost openness and a spirit of cooperation. The goal of fighting fairly is not to win or lose an argument but to work together to find solutions that are acceptable to both. Clearly, if one partner loses, both lose.

AWARE item 8.

In order to end an argument, it is better to give in. (False)

4. Say What You Really Mean. As conflict increases, we often fail to say what we really mean. We may agree on issues when we don't really want to accommodate. We think we do this to protect the other person's feelings, but we are also protecting ourselves from pain or embarrassment. The more we get in touch with and share how we really feel about an issue, the sooner we will be able to find a solution to the conflict.

Take, for example, the issue of cohabitation. Should the couple move in together or wait until marriage to live together? One partner may feel positive about cohabiting while the other might feel ambivalent, seeing both the positive and the negative consequences. Because cohabitation is a complex issue, it can be useful for the couple to write down the pros and cons: "I love him," "Mom and Dad will be mad," "I'm afraid I'll have to support him financially, and I can't even support myself now." After listing the pros and cons, the ambivalent individual can more clearly see why she or he is feeling undecided. The next important step is to share this clearly with the other person.

5. Avoid Accusations and Attacks. When we are accused, we tend to react either by accusing the other person of something or by withdrawing. "You" statements are implicit or explicit signals of attack: "You make me mad," "You always do that," or "It's all your fault." Most people become defensive and angry in response to "you" statements.

6. Own Your Own Feelings First. Instead of attacking with "you" statements, we can use "I" statements: "I feel hurt," "I feel rejected," or "I feel disappointed." Although the difference between saying "I" and saying "you" may seem small, it is significant. When we use "I," we clearly point out that something is wrong in the relationship and we are simply putting the issue on the table for discussion. "I" statements indicate that the other person is innocent until proven guilty, rather than vice versa.

7. Always Check Out Your Perceptions. Miscommunication is often the catalyst for disagreements. We shouldn't assume that we know what is going on until we have talked with the other person. Also, we shouldn't try to guess what the other person is thinking or feeling. It is our responsibility to ask.

8. State Your Wishes and Requests Clearly and Directly.
Dogs and cats often do a better job of communicating their needs than humans do. Because we are afraid of being turned down or rejected, we often do not directly say what we want. One common approach is to ask a leading question, one that hints at the desired result without directly asking for it. For example, if we wanted to go to a movie we might ask, "Wouldn't you like to see that movie tonight?" The indirect approach may work sometimes, but we should not rely on it to get us what we want. It is okay to ask for what you want.

9. Never Use Affection to Smooth Over a Disagreement.
People sometimes use affection as a tool or a weapon in an argument. When we use affection to get our mate to agree with us, the underlying issue or conflict often remains unresolved.

10. Repeat the Message You Think You Received.

Active listeners let others know that they correctly heard what was said. John Crosby calls this process "football": "You can't throw the ball (the message) back to your partner until you prove to your partner that you caught the ball (the message) he or she threw to you."

Active listeners don't repeat the message verbatim; instead they restate it in their own words to show their partner that they understand it. Active listening does three valuable things: it forces us to listen to one another; it slows down reaction time, which keeps the discussion calmer and more rational; and it helps get the message across.

11. Refuse to Fight Dirty. Dirty fighters lose the battle before they begin the attack. They prove their inability to deal positively and fairly with the situation. Here are four especially dirty fighting techniques:

- *Gunnysacking.* This is a tactic in which people stuff their true feelings into a deep sack and do not let the other person know what they are really feeling. The problem is that the gunnysack can hold only so much. When the sack overflows, it all "hangs out," and gunnysackers may verbally or physically attack the other person.

- *Passive-aggressive behavior.* Like gunnysackers, people using passive-aggressive behavior pretend to agree or act like everything is okay when in fact they really disagree with what is happening. People who act this way for some time eventually tend to become hostile and aggressive.

- *Rapid-fire questioning.* Rapid-fire questioning is an adversarial technique often used by police and lawyers to confuse a suspect or witness. People who use adversarial techniques in their job may try the same approach in their relationship, but such techniques do not build intimate relationships or resolve conflicts.

- *Verbal abuse and physical abuse.* Name-calling, yelling, pouting, and sulking all belong in the category of dirty-fighting techniques. Physical abuse is unacceptable. Neither of these approaches helps resolve a conflict.

12. Resist Giving the Silent Treatment. Refusing to talk—the silent treatment—is an attempt to get even with or manipulate others. Shutting out the other emotionally in the hope that the partner will give in is a form of psychological torture. This approach rarely resolves conflict. Disagreements do not go away by themselves. They may lie dormant for a while, but they will eventually resurface, often in a less manageable form than before. The shut-out partner's anger and frustration will also tend to increase, even though that may not be the intent of the partner who refuses to argue.

13. Focus on the Issue and Focus on the Present. Constructive arguments focus on the here-and-now and stay on the topic. Arguments that leap from one issue to another accomplish very little.

Bringing up the past usually is a ploy for placing blame and it usually makes things worse. In a fair fight, the relevant question is not "Where have we been?" but "Where are we going from here?"

AWARE item 9.
Bringing up the past often creates more conflict. (True)

14. Call "Time-Out" and "Foul." When verbal interchanges get too intense, a time-out can be useful. Its length depends on how emotionally agitated the participants are. Sometimes an hour is sufficient; sometimes it may take a day. Time-outs shouldn't last too long, however, because one or both persons may refuse to deal with the issue again.

Another helpful tool in a conflict is calling "foul" when fair-fighting rules are broken. If one person brings up the past or uses a dirty-fighting technique, call a "foul." This gives both partners a chance to calm down and think things through before trying again to resolve the disagreement.

15. Use Humor and Comic Relief. It is often just as useful to laugh as to cry. In a similar vein, it is better to laugh than to yell. People in an argument usually look and sound pretty foolish to an objective, calm third party. In a conflict, we need to step back, look at the situation from a new perspective, and laugh at ourselves if possible. However, sarcasm or laughing at the other person rarely helps resolve the dispute.

A useful form of humor for families is incongruity humor—the things that don't fit together logically—rather than on blaming others or putting them down. For example, a divorce court judge laughs when he tells of listening for three hours to a divorcing couple and their attorneys argue over who was to have possession of a nine-foot-long metal pipe. The judge tried to help the couple see the humor of the situation, but she was unsuccessful. Partners who can't laugh together, unfortunately, are often partners in deep trouble.

16. Always Go for Closure. Closure is the resolution of an issue. Try to bring the disagreement to an end as soon as possible. Letting an argument drag on increases the likelihood of gunnysacking, passive-aggressive behavior, or the silent treatment. The sooner people reach genuine agreement, the better. Resolution lets the feelings of bonding and respect return in the relationship.

> *Think about situations where you or others have used these constructive approaches to fair fighting. The more you can use these approaches, the greater the chances that you will get conflict resolved and the closer you will end up feeling about the relationship.*

Ten Steps for Resolving Conflict

We're all aware of conflicts in our world that people simply have not resolved successfully. Let's look at a real-life example. This family does a good job of communicating with one another and works out a solution to their conflict on which both can agree. Eileen James, and her oldest son, Marcus, age 16, disagree with Marcus's curfew. Marcus came home very late, and Eileen is upset. Let's analyze how they successfully approach this conflict, using ten steps that have proven useful for people in conflict in the past.

1. Set a Time and a Place for Discussion. It is important to focus on the issue, without distractions. In this situation, before lunch the next day, Eileen finds Marcus listening to a CD in his room.

"Can we sit down this evening and talk about curfew hours?" she says.

"I've got a baseball game tonight," he replies.

They settle on 8 p.m. Monday evening in the living room. Marcus's two younger siblings will be at a track meet with their father, so Eileen and Marcus will have some uninterrupted time to work things out.

2. Define the Problem or Issue of Disagreement. It is important to clarify the problem so that both parties know they are talking about the same thing.

> *"Marcus, I was upset with you because you were out way past the time you said you would be home," Eileen explains.*

> *"You weren't mad because I was out with Jeff and Brian?" Marcus asks.*

> *"No," she replies.*

> *"I thought you didn't like them," he says.*

> *"No, I think they're great kids. I especially like Jeff's sense of humor, and Brian's always so polite and thoughtful around me. I was simply upset because you said you would be home at 11 p.m. and you came home at 12:30."*

3. Talk About How Each of You Contributes to the Problem. Mutual sharing of responsibility eliminates finger pointing. *Remember:* When you point your finger at somebody, there are three fingers pointing back at yourself. When there is a problem in a relationship, it is rarely exclusively one person's fault.

> *"Okay, I understand," Marcus continues. "And you're right. I did say 11. We were just having such a great time talking in Brian's basement that I didn't know what time it was."*

> *"Well, maybe I didn't make it clear why it was so important for me to know where you were", Eileen admitted.*

AWARE item 10.
When there is a problem in a relationship, usually both people are at fault.
(True)

4. List Past Unsuccessful Attempts to Resolve the Issue.
Reviewing failed approaches helps you clarify the need to come up with new solutions.

"This happened two weeks ago, Marcus. You remember?"

"Yes, Mom."

"And, wait. It happened just last week. Remember how upset I was then?"

"Yes, I thought you were going to flip," he smiles.

"I guess I was a bit nutty then," she laughs. "You know, we didn't really sit down and talk after it happened. I guess you just ended up going your way, and I was too busy with other things and went my way."

"Why do you get so upset, Mom? Don't you trust me?"

"Oh, yes, I trust you. I am just afraid something has happened to you."

5. Brainstorm New Ways to Resolve the Conflict. List all possible solutions, even ideas that may seem silly or strange. Be creative. Remember, there are no right or wrong answers. Do not evaluate any ideas while brainstorming because first you need ideas to evaluate. The next step is discussing and evaluating ideas.

"Well, we've got to find a solution to this problem," Eileen said. "Let's do some brainstorming."

"Okay, Mom. You could ground me at home after dark."

"Good thinking!" Eileen chuckled. "What else?"

"Or you could go buy some sleeping pills, and when I'm out past curfew you could knock yourself out with them and have pleasant dreams."

"What about if I bought you a new watch with a beeper on it, and set to go off at 10:30 p.m.?"

What if you just set my curfew for 1 a.m.? I'd start to get tired by then and be ready to come home."

Mother and son continued brainstorming in this way for quite a while, clearly enjoying each other's company. Finally, they got a list of ten options.

6. Discuss and Evaluate Possible Solutions. Talk about what each of you could do to help solve the problem.

"Mom, 11 p.m. is really too early. All my friends get to stay out till midnight or 1."

"Well, I suppose I could loosen up on you a bit. But I worry so."

"I could call you to let you know where I am and that I'm okay."

"That sure would help."

7. Agree on One Solution to Try. Start with the idea you both think would most likely resolve the issue, and just give it a try. Mother and son settled on a midnight curfew and agreed that Marcus would call to let Eileen know where he was.

8. Agree on How Each Individual Will Work Toward This Solution. Discuss specifically, and possibly write down, what each of you will do to help resolve this conflict.

"Okay, let's both write down our responsibilities," Eileen said. "I need to make it very clear for you, so I'll say, 'I would like Marcus to be home on school nights by 9 p.m. and on weekends by midnight.'"

"I can go along with that, but sometimes I would like to stay out longer—like, when Brian and Jeff and I are having a great time over at one of their houses. Could I call you before midnight and let you know what I'm up to and get some more time?"

"Okay, as long as I know where you are and that you're safe, I can live with that."

9. Set Up Another Meeting to Discuss Your Progress. Agree on a time and place to talk about your progress in resolving the issue:

"Let's go out to dinner in a month to talk about how we're doing on this, Marcus. Don't worry, I'll buy!"

163

10. Reward Each Other As You Each Contribute Toward the Solution. Notice the little things the other person does along the way to reach a mutual resolution. Thank and praise her or him for the effort.

"Marcus, it was nice of you to call last night at 11:30."

"I appreciate you giving me an extra hour and a half, Mom. We were right in the middle of that game, and I was winning."

How did this mother and son resolve a potentially destructive conflict? By listening to each other respectfully, by speaking clearly about what each wished to have happen, and by not blaming each other, by being honest and appreciative toward one another. In short, they treated each other with love and kindness, the way healthy families do.

You might find it useful to go back and answer the AWARE questions at the beginning of this chapter one more time. Once you understand the key principles in successfully resolving conflicts, you're well on your way. The next step is to put these principles into practice in your everyday life.

Role
Relationships

> ❝ How you share
> your roles, will
> shape how you
> achieve your goals. ❞
>
> DR. D. H. OLSON

Aware Quiz

Who's the Boss?

Circle True or False

1 Traditional female roles are viewed as less important than working outside the home.　　　　　　　　　　　T or F

2 The husband should be just as willing as the wife is to adapt in marriage.　　　　　　　　　　　　　　T or F

3 Men often get paid more than women for the same job.　　T or F

4 It is just as acceptable for the man to stay home and care for the children as it is for the woman to do so.　　　　T or F

5 A woman's career can be just as important as a man's.　　T or F

6 Women should be able to keep their birth name after marriage.　T or F

7 The tasks a man or woman does around the house should be based on interests and skills rather than on gender.　　　T or F

8 Husbands should share household duties equally with their wives.　T or F

9 The husband should have the final word on important decisions.　T or F

10 Egalitarian decision making takes more work, but it is more satisfying.　　　　　　　　　　　　　　　T or F

Please complete the QUIZ before reading the chapter.

In recent decades, roles have become much less rigid for both men and women. Some men enjoy cooking, some women like mowing the lawn—and nobody likes to clean the bathroom. To gain a better understanding of roles, let's look at where men and women have been historically, and where they are today.

Although it may seem as if women have come a long way since the 1960's, the reality is that it's still a man's world. Traditionally, men were expected to support their families financially. And, because our society equates money with power, men were therefore, expected to be the primary decision makers.

Today most women also work outside the home. They work because they need to, want to, or a combination of both. But men's work typically still receives more respect and better pay. This creates an ongoing imbalance of power between men and women, both at work and in the home. For married couples, this imbalance can lead to a breakdown in intimacy. In essence, we really do not like or enjoy being around someone who is our boss. The power "a boss" has over us makes us uncomfortable, and these feelings are a barrier to developing a sense of closeness.

What is Gender Bias?

We live in a gender-biased culture that places more value on men and on the work they do than on women. To gain a better understanding of how we are programmed to think in stereotypes, read the following puzzle and answer the question at the end.

A Puzzle.

> A man is driving down the road with his son and he gets into an automobile accident. The father was not injured, but the son was taken by ambulance to the hospital. When the son goes into the operating room, the surgeon says, "I can't operate on this patient, he's my son!"
>
> How can this be possible?

Researchers who study language are quick to point out that the very words we speak are loaded in favor of males. Take a look at Box 9-1 to see what we mean.

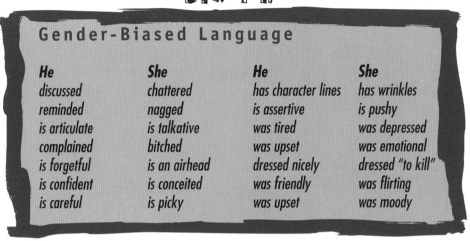

Box 9-1.

Gender-Biased Language

He	She	He	She
discussed	chattered	has character lines	has wrinkles
reminded	nagged	is assertive	is pushy
is articulate	is talkative	was tired	was depressed
complained	bitched	was upset	was emotional
is forgetful	is an airhead	dressed nicely	dressed "to kill"
is confident	is conceited	was friendly	was flirting
is careful	is picky	was upset	was moody

Source: Based in part on *Sex Differences in Human Communication* (p. 131) by Barbara Westbrook Eakins and R. Gene Eakins. Copyright © 1978 by Harper & Row, Publishers, Inc. Reprinted by permission of HarperCollins Publishers, Inc.

Devaluing the Women's Work

The work that women have traditionally done in our society is commonly not treated with respect or seen as being as valuable as men's work. Child care is often denigrated and considered something that anyone can do successfully. Housework often isn't considered "real" work at all because our culture defines work as something done for pay. This definition implies that family work is somehow inferior to paid work. In reality, however, family work is often more demanding, time-consuming, and important than jobs that people are paid to do.

A caring and appreciative husband once said: When I think of what my wife contributes to the world by caring so well for our three daughters, I'm really embarrassed at my modest accomplishments in life. Sally is genuinely needed by those kids. She keeps them alive and happy and healthy every day and they are great kids mainly because of her efforts.

Virginia Satir, a family therapist, coined the term "peoplemaking" to describe the importance and responsibility tied to the task of raising children. The focus on some jobs is making cars or televisions or computers. A parent's job is to make people, obviously not an easy task.

AWARE item 1.
Traditional female roles are viewed as less important than working outside the home. (True)

In addition to childrearing, housekeeping and home maintenance also take a significant amount of time out of the day. Even if both partners work outside the home, the woman is likely to do a majority of the housework. And researchers have found that women who work 30 hours or more per week outside the home are still likely to spend an average of five hours a day on housework. This leads to a basic inequity in many households, with many wives working longer and harder than their husbands. Such situations are not conducive to long-term marital happiness.

Women are often assigned the role of balancing schedules in the family. In fact, this is such a common challenge that countless news stories and magazine articles are written today on the issue of balance: "Balancing Work and Family," "The Difficult Juggling Act," and so forth. What exactly is involved in all this?

It means, for many working mothers, that they work The Second Shift, in the words of sociologist Arlie Hochshild. These chronically tired women often put in 16-hour days: working outside the home all day and then coming home to a second job (their family job) with which they get little help from their husbands.

> *I work eight hard hours teaching school. When I come home, it is time to fix dinner, and at night there's always some laundry to do and housecleaning and correspondence and what not. I hate to ask my husband to help, or the kids. They're always so busy also, and frankly when I do ask for help, they always have excuses. It's just easier to do it myself.*

Giving Men's Needs Priority

Because men's work is valued more in our culture, the husband's needs often come before the wife's. Moms are more likely than dads to juggle their schedules when a child is ill and can not go to school. Moms tend to worry more about the details of household management—if there's milk in the fridge, when the teacher needs to be called, whether a birthday gift needs to be purchased—even though moms often work just as many hours outside the home as dads.

Because husbands usually have the job that pays more and has higher social status, wives are more likely than husbands to follow their spouses from city to city in the quest for career advancement. This causes a good deal of disruption in the life of the person who is the follower, of course. Friendships may end and separation from other family members can be very painful.

Traditionally, women and children have taken the man's name in our culture. The woman's identity may even disappear completely when she becomes "Mrs. John Smith." Some might argue that this is "not a big deal," but the legitimate question remains: "Why don't men change their names when they marry?"

Women often adapt to the man's life, and yet these adaptations can be very difficult. For example, one woman we know followed her husband as he attained one graduate degree after another, and then bounced from one job to another. She dutifully enrolled in college at each stop on his career adventure, taking a class here and there while juggling childrearing and housework. When we met her she had amassed 178 hours of college credits from ten different institutions, but they still didn't add up to what should have been a 125- or 128-hour bachelor's degree. Each college had different rules; a course that counted toward a degree at one school was looked upon with disfavor at another. This woman was caught between inflexible institutions and a husband who would not recognize her needs to develop her own interests and skills.

The emphasis our society places on women's adapting to men's lives, rather than vice versa, says that men are more important in our society. It also is a tremendous waste of human potential. We cannot afford to support half of the people in our society in their quest for growth and neglect the other half. Finally, marriages in which one partner is allowed to fly while the other is stifled tend to be unhappy marriages.

AWARE item 2.
The husband should be just as willing as the wife is to adapt in marriage. (True)

Unequal Pay for Equal Work

Our society places enormous importance—for better or worse—on money. One of the ways we show people how much we value them is by how much we pay them for their work. Women today with four years of college education still earn less than men with only a high-school diploma. Also, for the same jobs women only earn 80 percent of what a man earns. Money buys power in our society, and in the home. If a wife feels ignored, neglected, or dominated by a more powerful husband, this can have sad consequences in terms of marital satisfaction.

AWARE item 3.
Men often get paid more than women for the same job. (True)

How Our Culture Shapes Our Roles

As human beings we like to think that we are free to do as we please, that we're free to create our own world to live in as we see fit. In actuality, however, the culture in which we live shapes our values, beliefs, and behaviors to a great degree, and it is difficult to swim against the mainstream.

Young adults often try to fight the dominant culture by dressing differently, talking differently, listening to different music, and so forth. But they often fall into the trap of all being different in the same way. It isn't really a significant break with mainstream culture when so many in the youth subculture are wearing buzz cuts, dying their hair orange, wearing certain clothes or whatever else is the current fad. This basically says, "Let's be different, but let's all be different together."

Our gender roles and role relationships are also shaped by our culture. This shaping process starts at birth. Everyone knows that blue baby clothes are for boys and pink clothes are for girls. We talk about boy babies and girl babies differently: boy babies look big and strong and handsome to us; girl babies look dainty and precious and cute. We give boy babies strong- and authoritative- and intelligent-sounding names: "John" and "Justin" and "Jason." We give girl babies gentle and approachable names: "Ashley" and "Jennifer" and "Alyssa." We even tend to talk to boy and girl babies differently. "Sex-appropriate" toys help shape behavior as boys and girls grow. We give girls dolls to help them become nurturing mothers. We give boys tools, guns and trucks.

We have gotten to the point at which "housewife" and "homemaker" are problem words. Many women feel forced to pursue work outside the home to gain respect from others. Maintaining a happy home and nurturing children are just not enough for many women. That is a dramatic change from the 1950s when home and family were common. And yet, the changes in women's lives look much more dramatic than the changes we have seen in men's lives. Countless women are involved in work for pay outside the home. But how many househusbands do you know?

Role reversals are not at all common for men. Women have taken on a job outside the home while retaining most of their responsibilities inside the home. Men have not been as willing to increase their level of involvement in the home.

Why? One important reason is that men's work has historically had higher status than women's work in our society. Women can achieve higher status by working outside the home, but why would men want to lose their status by becoming househusbands?

This attitude is unfortunate because one's sex does not dictate one's abilities. One husband chuckles, "I think my wife makes the mistake of thinking sometimes that just because I am a man I am automatically a handyman. Actually, I'm absolutely horrible at fixing things." Men aren't born handymen. And women, for that matter, aren't always the more nurturing spouse. "I'm just better at reading stories and doing artwork and homework and giving baths," one father explained. "Andrea gets too impatient, so I do most of the child care when we come home from work." The role one plays in the family should be decided not on the basis of one's sex but on one's interests and abilities.

AWARE item 4.

It is just as acceptable for the man to stay home and care for the children as it is for the woman to do so. (True)

How Our Family Shapes Our Roles

One important way we learn roles in life is by observing and imitating important people, often our mother and father. Their behaviors serve as a guide. As a child if we see Mom cleaning the house and doing the grocery shopping, we learn, "This is what mothers do." When the father does the yard work and gets up on the roof to check for leaks, we think, "This is what fathers do."

Besides observation and imitation, roles are reinforced through communication: "Big boys don't cry!" "Only sissies play with dolls." "You're such a good girl to help Mommy wash the dishes." What we see at home is not the only influence on our role behavior, however. Many of today's nontraditional mothers and fathers grew up in families that were very traditional. What accounts for this change?

An Evolving Society

People who grow up in very rigid families in which Mom always does "women's work" and Dad does "man's work" may behave very differently when they marry. There are many other role models in the world that we can choose to follow. Society is changing slowly and steadily, evolving into a more egalitarian model where more roles are shared.

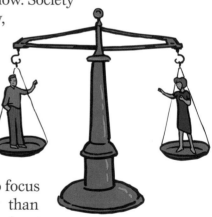

Family life is clearly not as predictable as it once was in terms of role relationships. Expectations for specific social positions, such as "mother" or "father," have shifted somewhat to focus on individual preferences rather than roles being determined only by one's age and sex. Look at Box 9-2 to see some of the changes we have experienced in society as we have moved from a traditional orientation to a more contemporary orientation.

Box 9-2.

Comparison of Traditional and Contemporary Dating and Marriage Patterns

Traditional	Contemporary
The man initiates dates.	Both women and men initiate dates.
The woman takes the man's last name.	The woman keeps her given name after marriage.
The couple live apart before marriage.	The couple cohabit before marriage.
No premarital sex.	Premarital sex is more common.
The wife supports the husband through school.	Both continue their educations.
Children are conceived after marriage.	The birth of a child might precede marriage.
The husband's work is the priority.	Both people work, and both may have careers.
Roles are rigid.	Roles are flexible.
The mother is responsible for the child.	Spouses share child care.
The husband initiates sex.	Both initiate sex.
The husband's friends become the couple's friends.	Both select the couple's friends.

Many people believe, however, that we have a long way to go in the quest for a society that does not dictate one's life course on the basis of one's sex. It is clear from Box 9-2, though, that there are dramatic differences between traditional gender-role behaviors and more contemporary patterns of behavior.

Increases in Women Working Outside the Home

Government statistics indicate clearly that a higher percentage of women—unmarried women, married women, and women with children—are working outside the home today than in past decades. Women seek employment for a variety of reasons, but basically because they have to work to support or help support their families and because they like to work.

Even though husbands tend to make more money than their wives, the wife's income can be absolutely critical to the family's survival. And in addition to pure and simple economics, women can receive a good deal of satisfaction working for pay (just as men do) and can feel bored or lonely staying at home all the time.

AWARE item 5.
A woman's career can be just as important as a man's. (True)

Changes in Dating and Marriage Patterns

As Box 9-2 illustrates, dating and marriage have evolved in recent decades, making the lives of many people quite different from the lives of their parents and grandparents. Women initiate dates today and are now feeling much of the same anxiety previously reserved for men: "Should I call him? Will he hang up on me? Does he think I'm attractive enough to go out with, or am I just kidding myself?" and so forth.

Many women, not wishing to submerge their identity totally in that of their husbands, are choosing to keep their birth name (their family-of-origin's name) after marriage. Some women keep their birth name and add their husband's family name. Some men take their wife's family name. There are many possible ways to deal with the issue of family names. This is an important subject for couples to talk about before marriage.

AWARE item 6.
Women should be able to keep their birth name after marriage. (True)

Both partners in these new egalitarian relationships are likely to continue their educations, for school is seen as an important source of financial security and satisfaction for both men and women. The couple might have a child before marrying. Both are likely to have jobs; both might even have the more engaging and challenging type of job we call a career.

Roles are flexible in these new egalitarian relationships. Around the house and in the working world, partners do what they like to do, what they're comfortable doing, what they're good at doing, and what they negotiate together to be a fair division of labor. In sum, people can consciously choose what roles they are going to play in the relationship, rather than the roles being dictated by society.

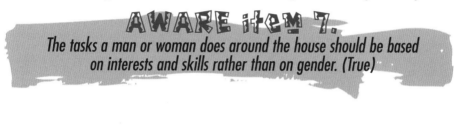

AWARE item 7.

The tasks a man or woman does around the house should be based on interests and skills rather than on gender. (True)

Housework: Too Often a Woman's Responsibility

Even when both partners work outside the home, the woman often ends up doing most of the housework. Women are successfully making the transition to working in the job market, but men aren't reciprocating as well on the home front. Housework, tends to be monotonous, highly repetitive, and is "never done."

There is considerable evidence, however, that couples with more egalitarian relationships tend to have better relationships. The more a couple is able to share leadership, decision making, and tasks around the house, the happier they tend to be. In fact, one way a husband can show he loves his wife is to do his share of the housework.

Researchers have found that household tasks are one of the most common reasons for disagreements between couples. Battles over who does what, and how well they are doing it, are quite common in most marriages.

Mary was married to a male chauvinist. They both worked full time, but he never did anything around the house and certainly not any housework. That, he declared, was woman's work.

But one evening Mary arrived home from work to find the children bathed, a load of wash in the washing machine, and another in the dryer, dinner on the stove, and a beautifully set table, complete with flowers.

She was astonished, and she immediately wanted to know what was going on. It turned out that Charlie, her husband, had read a magazine article that suggested that working wives would be more romantically inclined if they weren't so tired from having to do all the housework in addition to holding down a full-time job.

The next day, she couldn't wait to tell her friends at the office.

"How did it work out?" one of them asked.

"Well, it was a great dinner," Mary said. "Charlie even cleaned up, helped the kids with their homework, folded the laundry, and put everything away."

"But what about afterward?" her friends wanted to know.

"It didn't work out," Mary said. "Charlie was too tired."

Leadership Patterns in Relationships

Power in a marriage can be divided in four basic ways:

- a **husband-dominated power pattern,** in which the man is more often the leader in the family

- a **wife-dominated power pattern,** in which the woman is more often the leader in the family

- an **egalitarian power pattern,** in which the partners make decisions together in most areas

- an **independent power pattern,** in which each spouse has about equal authority but in different areas of life. They essentially make decisions in their particular domains independently of each other.

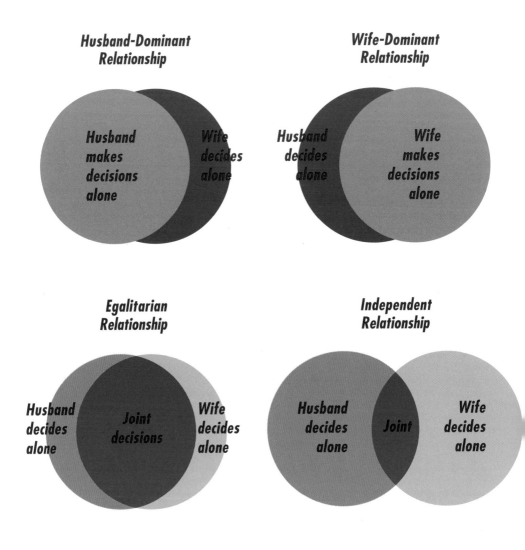

Figure 9-1.
Four Types of Leadership

Husband-Dominant Relationship

Husband makes decisions alone

Wife decides alone

Wife-Dominant Relationship

Husband decides alone

Wife makes decisions alone

Egalitarian Relationship

Husband decides alone

Joint decisions

Wife decides alone

Independent Relationship

Husband decides alone

Joint

Wife decides alone

Egalitarian: shared authority and joint decision making in most areas

Independent: about equal authority, but in different areas of life

These four basic patterns of power are illustrated in Figure 9-1. In the early stages of a relationship, there can be a great deal of instability as the couples struggle to work out the balance of power. As time passes, the partners assert themselves to establish some power in the relationship. A **male- or female-dominated relationship,** with one person leading and the other following, is difficult to maintain. Eventually the dominant one may tire of leading and the submissive one may tire of following. This can facilitate change to another type of power sharing.

In an **egalitarian relationship,** the sharing of decisions and tasks causes a better power balance in the family system. The partners are relatively equal, and couples with children often encourage the children to share in decision making, especially as the children become older.

In an **independent relationship,** one spouse may have most of the power in one area, such as the home, whereas the other spouse may have most of the power in another area, such as outside the home. Both perceive the relationship to be relatively equal in power on the whole, because both areas of power are perceived to be important.

AWARE item 9.
The husband should have the final word on important decisions. (False)

Benefits of Egalitarian Relationships

Creating an egalitarian relationship is not easy. It takes a great deal of positive communication between the partners, but the benefits of such a relationship are clear. Partners in egalitarian relationships:

- Tend to be more involved with and happier with each other.

- Accept more responsibility for each other's growth and well-being and are less likely to blame each other.

- Tend to make better decisions because their decisions are based on two perspectives (or even more, if relatively mature children participate) rather than just one.

Many people come from families in which one person dominates the other family members. It is often difficult for them to understand the benefits of a more fair distribution of power in the family. Their attitude may be "My dad bossed everybody around when I was a kid, so now it's my turn!" Sometimes it takes months or even years before a couple learns how to relate to each other on an equal basis. Some couples never reach this point. The goal, is well worth the effort, however, for the benefits of living together as equals are considerable.

American society is founded upon the ideal of democracy. In more than two hundred years, our country has yet to create a perfect form of democracy, but the ideal remains valid. Similarly, couples will find it difficult to create a genuinely fair and open relationship with each other, but moving positively in the right direction is well worth the effort.

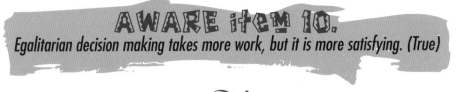

AWARE iteM 10.
Egalitarian decision making takes more work, but it is more satisfying. (True)

We hope you have enjoyed reading about role relationships in families in this chapter. Go back to the beginning, and answer the questions on the Aware Quiz on Who's the Boss again. See if you've increased your awareness of role-relationship issues.

Affection
and Sexuality

> **Friends Misrepresent sex; Parents repress sex; The Culture exploits sex.**
>
> LETTY COTTIN POGREBIN

Aware Quiz

Expressing Affection

Circle True or False

1 Men and women are significantly more alike than different. T or F

2 A "real man" has manly masculine traits. T or F

3 We learn we are boys or girls based on how others react to us. T or F

4 Sex and sexuality are shown realistically and factually in the media. T or F

5 The media tends to focus on women only as sexual objects. T or F

6 Sex education encourages young people to become sexually active. T or F

7 Married couples find it easy to discuss sex. T or F

8 Decisions about family planning or birth control are easy to make. T or F

9 A good sexual relationship is often the outcome of a good emotional relationship between partners. T or F

10 Men tend to focus on sexual intimacy as a way to get close; women tend to be interested in sexual intimacy after they feel close. T or F

Please complete the QUIZ before reading the chapter.

Are the Sexes Really "Opposite?"

Traditionally, men and women have been thought of as opposites. The focus has been on how very different the sexes are, rather than on their readily apparent similarities. The logical problem with this line of thinking is that opposites cannot possess the same traits or qualities, and yet men and women share a remarkable collection of similar behaviors. Women can be, in family therapist Virginia Satir's words, both tough and tender. Likewise, men have both the capacity to be strong and resilient when the situation demands it and the capacity to be nurturing. Just picture a new father proudly and gently holding his baby.

The main problem with the view that men and women are opposite is that it is simply not true. Men and women are significantly more alike-physically, hormonally and psychologically-than they are different. Compare men and women with any other living thing and you'll notice the remarkable similarities!

In terms of levels of aggression and other social behaviors, these slight differences are most likely the result of social learning and expectations by our culture. When certain behaviors and characteristics are labeled as feminine or masculine, young boys and girls learn to suppress their natural traits that "belong to the opposite sex." As a result, some of our common abilities and uniquenesses are lost.

Though men and women have obvious physical differences, it is not particularly helpful to over emphasize those differences, because our capacity as humans to adapt our behavior to different environments is so great. Today there are female marines and male kindergarten teachers, female prosecuting attorneys and male nurses, female governors and male secretaries.

It is therefore beneficial to think of female and male human beings as more alike than different. Especially in the areas that really count—our emotions—we aren't really opposites at all. Physically we're somewhat different from each other, but where it counts deep down we have remarkably similar capacities: the capacity for loving, the capacity for courage and cowardice, the capacity to succeed and the capacity to fail. For this reason, the description "opposite" sex doesn't make much sense.

AWARE item 1.
Men and women are significantly more alike than different. (True)

Femininity and Masculinity: Changing Definitions

When we believe that some characteristic we possess is generally considered to belong to the "opposite" sex, we tend to suppress that trait. But in reality, each of us possesses most of the traits that are traditionally assigned to the other sex.

The terms *femininity* and *masculinity* used to have very clear meanings in American culture, but today the definitions have broadened considerably. In the past, women were expected to act feminine, and that meant taking a backseat to men. For their part, men were expected to be masculine: strong, capable, aggressive. The roles were clearly defined. Watch almost any cowboy movie from the 1950s. It will be very clear what masculinity and femininity meant in that period of American history.

Today women can both lead and follow. Men, too. Masculinity and femininity as words have lost much of their power, influence, and scope. We still value men who look strong and capable but our society also needs men who are nurturing and sensitive, men who are balanced human beings.

Times have changed, and we believe these changes have been for the better. We can still enjoy the wonderful physical differences between men and women. *Vive la difference!* And yet, as a society we are learning not to **over emphasize** those differences. Insisting on men who can only be tough and women who can only be tender handicaps both genders. It robs each of us of our human capacities. Fortunately, what were masculine traits and feminine traits 30 years ago have become *human* traits.

AWARE item 2.
A "real man" has mainly masculine traits. (False)

Learning—and Understanding— Gender Stereotypes

At birth, our gender is assigned to us based on our anatomy, but our culture seems to over emphasize gender stereotypes. At birth babies are wrapped in pink blankets or blue blankets. We are called "cute little baby girls" or "big strong boys". As preschoolers we become adept at doing "girl things" (like dolls) if we are girls and "boy things" (like trucks) if we are boys.

Clearly, as the following anecdote shows, we also start stereotyping each other at a very young age.

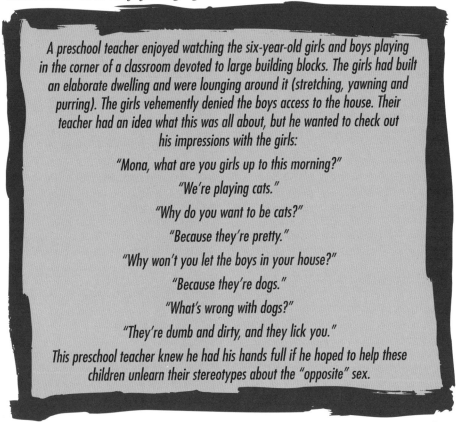

A preschool teacher enjoyed watching the six-year-old girls and boys playing in the corner of a classroom devoted to large building blocks. The girls had built an elaborate dwelling and were lounging around it (stretching, yawning and purring). The girls vehemently denied the boys access to the house. Their teacher had an idea what this was all about, but he wanted to check out his impressions with the girls:

"Mona, what are you girls up to this morning?"

"We're playing cats."

"Why do you want to be cats?"

"Because they're pretty."

"Why won't you let the boys in your house?"

"Because they're dogs."

"What's wrong with dogs?"

"They're dumb and dirty, and they lick you."

This preschool teacher knew he had his hands full if he hoped to help these children unlearn their stereotypes about the "opposite" sex.

Society is very efficient at making sure we learn its gender stereotypes well. It has been argued that our devotion to these stereotypes peaks when we are teenagers. As adults, we spend the rest of our lives unlearning our stereotypic thinking. It may take us a lifetime to realize that people are magnificently adaptable and that putting them in gender-role boxes only makes them less than they can genuinely be.

The gender we are assigned at birth, based on anatomy, shapes our destiny in countless ways. In our culture people's responses to us are based on our gender assignment. We learn we are boys or girls—and what that means—based on how people react to us. And though these influences often make little sense to us or our families, they can be very difficult to escape.

AWARE item 3.

We learn we are boys or girls based on how others react to us. (True)

Sexuality and Popular Culture

Sex is everywhere in American society today. On television, in the movies, in the newspapers, in books and magazines, on billboards, in store windows, in our daily conversations…wherever you go you are likely to encounter a message with a sexual connotation. Advertisers believe sex sells, and our American media overflows with a sexual cascade.

You might try an experiment: carry a notebook with you and jot down each time you see or hear something sexual. It won't take long to fill several pages.

In the past, sex was not everywhere. Discussion of sexual issues was a cultural taboo, and sexuality was relegated to hidden corners and dark alleys. Sex was concealed, and sex education was nonexistent. Today, we find ourselves in a curious position: sex is everywhere, but sex education to help young people survive in our sexually drenched society is under continuous attack.

Learning About Sex

Unfortunately, the media has become more important than the family, the school, and the religious institution in influencing the sexual attitudes and behaviors of young people. In our dialogues with young people in our classes for more than 25 years we have found only a tiny percentage of students who believe their parents really taught them very much about sex and sexuality while they were growing up. A typical comment: "Mom or dad couldn't talk about sex with me! They got too embarrassed."

Parents, who didn't receive any formal sex education themselves, are often squeamish about the subject and incapable of educating their children. Schools and churches, both natural places for sound sex education to occur, consider this subject too politically hot to handle. This abdication of responsibility by three of our society's most important institutions—families, educational institutions, and religious institutions—leaves a huge vacuum. The media fills this vacuum with its own brand of sex "education," which tends to be heavy on soap operas. Because the media's focus is entertainment rather than information, their depiction of sex and sexuality is not usually realistic, and can often genuinely damage people's lives.

Another source of "education" for society's young is their peer group. The peer group learns what it teaches from the media and from the street. Rather than providing trusted mentors to guide young people through one of life's most challenging journeys, we leave the young to their own devices. That method of instruction can best be described as the pooling of ignorance.

The peer groups generally are not good sources of factual and objective information. Also the entertainment industry's goal is to increase ratings and make money rather than to inform, educate, and guide the young in positive directions. If this is the situation of our society today then it should come as little surprise that this country has serious problems dealing with healthy sex education.

AWARE item 4.
Sex and sexuality are shown realistically and factually in the media. (False)

Exploitation of Humans As Sex Objects

Sexual images of women and, increasingly, of men are used to sell products. Companies know this tactic works, or they wouldn't spend millions of dollars on advertising that uses sex to sell. Unfortunately, these ads perpetuate myths that are damaging to both women and men. They negatively influence us, perpetuating the myth that what we look like is more important than who we are. For example, *Sports Illustrated* devotes a very small portion of it's magazine to women's sports, yet its annual swimsuit issue featuring women in bathing suits sells twice as many copies as its other issues.

"Don't be a cold fish," you might respond. "What's the big deal?" The problem is that most of the images of women shown in the media are sexual in nature, and these images subtly and steadily influence our basic beliefs about women. Rather than seeing women as people, we may begin to see them as sexual beings first, and human beings only incidentally. This infringes on women's rights as human beings to play multiple roles in life.

AWARE iTEM 5.
The media tends to focus on women only as sexual objects. (True)

Sex Education

Where do Americans get their sex education? The Janus Report on Sexual Behavior found that most people learn about sex "on the street" from their peers. Home ranks second as a source of sex education, followed by school and, rarely, place of worship.

Sex Education and Parents

Today most students receive some type of sex education before graduating from high school, but few are involved in relatively long-term, comprehensive sex education programs. Instead, the limited sex education programming offered in schools is usually short term and narrow in scope. Few children receive any information from their parents about sex, either. Even though most parents, teachers, and school administrators agree that adolescents need the knowledge necessary to make healthy, responsible choices about their sexual behavior, we avoid the subject like the plague in our society.

Researchers have found that more than 80 percent of American adults favor sex education. The Janus survey found, for example, that sex education is favored by 86 percent of the population and that 89 percent want courses for children age 12 and older to include birth control information. About 75 percent of adults want the courses to talk about homosexuality and abortion.

Arguments against sex education tend to focus on the notion that talking about sex in schools leads to increased sexual activity among the young. We have yet to see a credible scientific study that backs up this belief. Such an argument also contradicts generally recognized educational principles. It assumes, essentially, that ignorance is bliss. If we were to apply the same argument to other aspects of the high-school curriculum, we would need to eliminate driver-education courses because talking about car wrecks could lead to students wanting to have car wrecks. Similarly, we would not talk about cigarettes or alcohol or drugs in health education classes because talking about these items would make students want to try them.

The fact of the matter is that all kinds of sex education is going on today. The problem is most sex education happens "on the street" and through the media. People who are genuinely on the side of young people—parents, teachers, school administrators, and religious educators—have a responsibility to also become involved in

sex education that is presented in a sound and responsible manner. If we do not provide good sex education, we allow young people to learn it on their own.

AWARE item 6.

Sex education encourages young people to become sexually active. (False)

Is Sex Education Effective?

Do sex-education programs work? A seven-year Mathtech Inc. study of nine programs around the country, concluded that sex-education programs must meet certain conditions if they are to be effective. Two of the nine programs studied were rated as being very successful: these programs had strong backing from parents and the local community; and the use of birth control increased because these programs were coupled with ready access to a health clinic. Graduates of sex-education programs were less permissive about nonmarital sex than were young people in control groups, according to the researchers.

A Minnesota-based high school program recorded 40 percent lower birth rates of teenagers in schools with health clinics. Of the adolescent mothers who used the clinics, 80 percent stayed in school, and repeat pregnancies were almost nonexistent. Follow-up contact was necessary in the programs, however, because teenagers are poor at remembering to use birth control. The Minnesota program experience supports other studies that have reported that only 14 percent of teenage girls use contraceptives the first time they have intercourse. In short, the availability of contraceptives does not lead teenagers to have sex. Researchers have found that 86 percent of the time, girls have intercourse for the first time without contraceptive protection.

A New Approach to Sex Ed

Box 10-1.

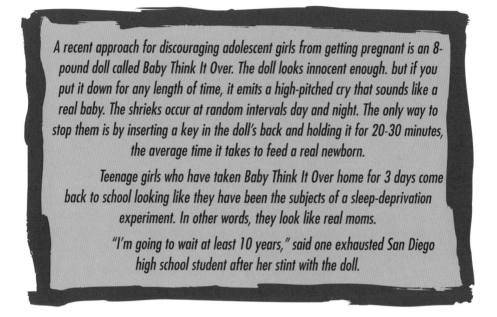

A recent approach for discouraging adolescent girls from getting pregnant is an 8-pound doll called Baby Think It Over. The doll looks innocent enough. but if you put it down for any length of time, it emits a high-pitched cry that sounds like a real baby. The shrieks occur at random intervals day and night. The only way to stop them is by inserting a key in the doll's back and holding it for 20-30 minutes, the average time it takes to feed a real newborn.

Teenage girls who have taken Baby Think It Over home for 3 days come back to school looking like they have been the subjects of a sleep-deprivation experiment. In other words, they look like real moms.

"I'm going to wait at least 10 years," said one exhausted San Diego high school student after her stint with the doll.

Source: from "Teens Need Dolls' Drastic Lessons" by David Grimes, 1994, Sarasota *Herald-Tribune.* Copyright © 1994 by David Grimes. Reprinted by permission of the Sarasota *Herald Tribune,* Sarasota, FL.

Sexual Attitudes

One of the ironies of life in the United States today is that although our society puts far too much emphasis on sex and sexuality, the subject is not often talked about openly in the context of an intimate relationship. We joke about sex. But we don't know how to talk about sex in an adult, rational manner. You'll rarely hear a genuinely grown-up, serious, thoughtful conversation about sex—even between married couples who regularly engage in sexual behavior with one another. Even married couples find it difficult to discuss their own sexual relationships.

AWARE item 7.
Married couples find it easy to discuss sex. (False)

Making Sexual Choices

Our inability to talk about sex in a straightforward way is problematic because we need to make many sexual choices based on our experience, attitudes, values, and knowledge. Our sex-saturated world is full of nonsense and fantasy. If you really believe that smoking cigarettes or drinking beer makes you more attractive to the other sex, as the advertisements would have you believe, you're going to be jeopardizing your health and happiness.

Because our attitudes on sexuality are influenced by less-than-accurate sources such as these, many of us are bound to have distorted and unrealistic views on important issues like these:

- *Becoming or continuing to be sexually active.* "The street" and the mass media are not good sources of information for making this consequential decision.

- *Practicing safe sex.* "The street" and the mass media are excellent sources for how to practice *unsafe* sex. How many times do you see the couple talking about their sexual histories first? Or talking about the very real possibility of a sexually transmissible disease? Rarely.

- *Family planning.* Contraception is rarely a topic of serious discussion in our society. Instead, for business reasons, the media glorifies sex but almost always fail to talk about its consequences.

Real-life discussions about sex are very difficult because we have little practice. Discussions about sexual issues embarrass us because they focus on intimate parts of our bodies. They also are difficult because they make us look deep-down at our moral values. Because partners are very likely to have different perspectives on morality, issues surrounding sexuality are challenging to discuss. For example, he believes that birth control is not needed. She wants to makes use of her college education and not have children for at least the first five years of marriage. They both love each other deeply, but do you think it will be easy for them to resolve this profound difference in thinking? Of course not.

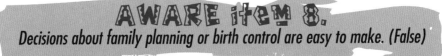

AWARE item 8.
Decisions about family planning or birth control are easy to make. (False)

Affection and Sexuality in Marriage

Sexuality is simply another aspect of loving a partner. It's important, but it's not everything. In married couples, a good sexual relationship is the outcome of a good emotional relationship. Couples who genuinely care for each other are good at expressing appreciation and affection. Smiles, hugs, pats on the back, compliments— these little emotional gifts we give each other every day cement our relationship together.

Before marriage, couples are typically pretty good at expressing positive feelings toward each other and can easily give compliments to their valued partner. Unfortunately, compliments often decrease dramatically after marriage. We begin to take our partner for granted. We often see or think about him or her less than before. The only way to maintain a good sexual relationship is to have a good emotional relationship.

"Sex doesn't begin Saturday night at 10:30 p.m.," one husband notes. "It begins Tuesday morning when I make her breakfast. And Wednesday evening when I give her a big hug for a wonderful dinner and when I do the dishes after the big hug. And Thursday afternoon when I take her mom to the doctor because she's got an important meeting at her office. And Friday evening when I listen to her describe the challenges she faces at the office and offer very tiny bits of gentle advice.

"I do all these things for her, and she does all kinds of things for me. And, if everything goes well emotionally for both of us throughout the week, then we have a better sexual relationship.

AWARE item 9.

A good sexual relationship is often the outcome of a good emotional relationship between partners. (True)

Gender Differences in Sexual Attitudes

It has been said that men give love to get sex and women give sex to get love. Although this statement is obviously an exaggeration, there is an element of truth in it. For many men, the physical act of sex can lead to emotional intimacy. For many women, it's just the opposite: emotional intimacy is the gateway to sexual intimacy.

Our culture in many ways socializes girls and women to be cooperative, and so wives tend to value closeness and emotional intimacy, which is established through open communication. Our culture still tends to emphasize competition in its socialization process for boys and men. Raised to compete in the world and hide their feelings because they might show weakness, men often have a difficult time talking openly and honestly about how they feel about things. These differences sometimes make it difficult for partners to genuinely connect with each other emotionally and sexually.

AWARE item 10.

Men tend to focus on sexual intimacy as a way to get close; women tend to be interested in sexual intimacy after they feel close. (True)

"Friends misrepresent sex," Letty Cottin Pogrebin has noted. "Parents repress sex. The culture exploits sex. How can children make sense of their bodies?"

And we would add, "How can couples make sense of their sexual relationship?"

The answer: positive, open, and honest communication.

❧

Now that you've finished Chapter 10, you might enjoy retaking the AWARE Quiz on "Affection and Sexuality" at the beginning of the chapter.

Financial Decisions

> **It's good to have money and things money can buy, but it's good to check once in a while and make sure you haven't lost the things money can't buy.**
>
> GEORGE HORACE LORIMER

Are You Financially Wise or Unwise?

Circle True or False

1 Financial issues are the most common source of problems within families and couple relationships.   T or F

2 People are often cautious or unwilling to discuss their income.   T or F

3 Young people often have unrealistic ideas of how much they will earn and how much things cost.   T or F

4 Credit cards often create financial problems for people and couples.   T or F

5 People have a style (spending or saving) of managing money that is difficult to change.   T or F

6 When dating, it is generally a good idea for couples to share the expenses.   T or F

7 People often spend more than they earn.   T or F

8 Creating a budget can keep you out of financial struggles.   T or F

9 People often have a difficult time creating a budget and sticking to it.   T or F

10 Establishing a good credit history is very important for your financial future.   T or F

Please complete the QUIZ before reading the chapter.

Money Problems

Regardless of how much money you make, financial issues are the most common source of problems for both individuals and families. In fact, one group of researchers found that 37 percent of all the married couples in their study believed money was the number one problem in their marriage.

AWARE item 1.
Financial issues are the most common source of problems within families and couple relationships. (True)

Money: A Taboo Topic

Adults generally do not like to talk about money, especially how much they earn. Most of us grow up in families where money and personal income are not openly discussed. And most of us continue this approach when we marry. In the dating phase, couples are more likely to talk about their past relationships than their financial situations. Paul, for example, would probably be more likely to tell Kelley about his past girlfriends than about his credit card balance or bounced checks. He knows some women have been attracted to him because of his job, but will be concerned if they know how much money he owes on his overextended credit cards.

Most young people haven't thought much about budgeting, especially if they are still living with their parents. Most parents shield their offspring from the grim realities that money problems bring. Parents often believe they are doing their kids a favor by letting them enjoy their high school and college years. But when reality strikes, people are too often into heavy debt. Money matters demand the attention of couples—whether they like it or not—and researchers have found that finances are the most commonly discussed and argued about topic after marriage.

AWARE item 2.
People are often cautious or unwilling to discuss their income. (True)

Unrealistic Expectations about Finances

Most young people have unrealistic expectations about how much money they can expect to earn and how much things cost. For that matter, older people aren't really all that good at estimating, either.

If older people have trouble keeping track of their income and expenses, imagine the difficulties younger people face. Because we generally don't talk about how much money we make, younger people don't have an accurate picture of how much income they can expect when they begin their life in the workplace. And because we also don't go into detail about our expenses in our daily conversations, younger people only learn through experience how much rent costs, how expensive utilities are, how large a damage deposit can be, and how difficult it can be to get some landlords to repair a broken toilet or patch a leaky roof. Likewise, the cost of groceries, medical bills, health insurance, and car maintenance and insurance can be genuinely shocking.

AWARE item 3.
Young people often have unrealistic ideas of how much they will earn and how much things cost (True).

Overreliance on Credit

Young people have a limited understanding of how much they will earn and how much living independently costs. Overspending is a common problem for many, and overusing credit cards is a common problem.

Credit is a broad term that describes paying for goods, services, or money sold on trust over a period of time. Credit cards make it easy to overspend and to get into debt. And the high interest rates on credit-card balances (often 18% or more) which is generally double the rate of a bank loan (often 8-10%) can make it difficult for many borrowers to pay more than just the interest on their debt.

AWARE item 4.
Credit cards often create financial problems for people and couples. (True)

Spenders versus Savers

Becoming a couple means deciding together how to spend or save money. It is not surprising that conflict over money is common among couples. When it comes to spending and saving, individuals have a wide variety of personal styles, which can create considerable conflict between partners and in families. It's a good idea for couples to talk about their spending/saving patterns before marriage, but, most couples do not find out until after marriage how different their spending/saving styles are.

People can be placed on a continuum as to whether they are spenders or savers. On one end of the scale are the totally irresponsible spenders. On the other end of the scale are the penny-pinchers. Fortunately, most people are somewhere between the two extremes. Most of us successfully manage to balance our impulses to spend money with our need to save some for a rainy day. In couple relationships, the greater the differences in spending and saving styles, the greater the potential conflict.

Our personal style of managing money is difficult to change because it is closely tied to our basic orientation toward life in general. For example, someone may have grown up in poverty in a family that did not know where the next meal was coming from. To this person money literally means life, and hanging onto money can be almost an obsession. Because of this background, this individual will likely be very cautious about spending money throughout life.

Another person might find it difficult to make close connections with others. That person now spends a great deal of money buying gifts for loved ones and friends, treating people to dinner and shows, and sending cards to people on their birthdays and other special occasions. These expenditures add up, but this person sees the expense essential to feeling loved and connected to other people. "It's just money!" they might respond when asked about the checkbook balance.

These people are unlikely to change their orientation toward spending or saving very readily. Their views of money and its relation to life are almost built into their personalities. This is why it is so important to get a sense of a prospective mate's feelings about money before marriage. If you can not come to some kind of agreement on financial issues, this area can create a lot of future conflict.

AWARE item 5.
People have a style (spending or saving) of managing money that is difficult to change. (True)

Using Money for Power and Control

Money can be a means for gaining and maintaining power over a partner or other family members. Although decision-making power in a family or relationship is not based only on financial resources, they are a major factor. There is an old saying: "He or she who holds the purse strings calls the shots."

Researchers who study power in families have found that employed wives exert greater decision-making power in the home than unemployed wives. Wives have the greatest power when they are employed full-time, are employed in prestigious work, and make more money than their husbands.

Even in the dating phases of a relationship, the connection between money and power can be an important issue with which to contend. In earlier generations, men paid for dates: the flowers, the dinners, the entertainment were generally seen as the male's responsibility. Women, in the past, were responsible for being attractive and interested in the male.

Today the rules appear to be changing. Many young women, especially those who have jobs, insist on paying their fair share of the monetary costs of the date. "This way I don't have to feel obligated to him," one told us. This young woman's approach seems to us to be a good one. It helps to lessen the game-playing that goes on in a relationship and gives the woman more power to decide what is—and what is not—in her best interest.

No matter who pays for the date, the male or the female or both, it is important that couples learn to talk to each other openly about the meaning of money in the relationship and about the related issues of power.

AWARE item 6.

When dating, it is generally a good idea for couples to share the expenses. (True)

Education and Gender: Impact on Earnings

More than half the families in the United States are considered middle-income families. The U.S. Bureau of the Census currently defines the middle-income range as between $15,000 and $75,000 per year for a family of 4. Lower-income families make less than $15,000 per year, and upper-income families make more than $75,000 (Figure 11-1).

Distribution of Families by Income Level

According to recent U.S. Bureau of the Census figures, there is a large difference between the average income of males and that of females at all educational levels, with men making more at each level. The average American man working full-time earns approximately $37,000 a year, whereas the average American woman working full-time earns less than $25,000.

Having an education pays off financially. The Census Bureau reports that individuals with eight or fewer years of formal education in this country earn about $13,000 a year. Those with a high school diploma average about $29,000. People with a college degree average more than $49,000. The financial benefit of education is greater for white males than it is for females and other minority groups.

Salaries in fields traditionally dominated by women tend to be lower than those in fields traditionally dominated by men. And, women often drop out of the labor force for a few years to have and care for children, while men gain job-related experience and seniority by staying in the work force. This also negatively affects women's income.

Figure 11-1.
Income Level of U.S. Families

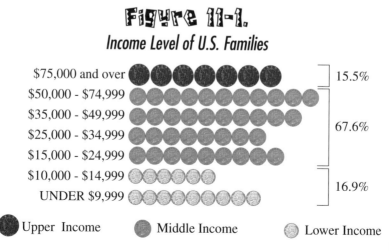

$75,000 and over — 15.5%

$50,000 - $74,999
$35,000 - $49,999
$25,000 - $34,999 — 67.6%
$15,000 - $24,999

$10,000 - $14,999
UNDER $9,999 — 16.9%

● Upper Income ● Middle Income ○ Lower Income

Too Much Spending, Not Enough Money

People often spend more than they earn. They do this by buying on credit. Many people act as if money in a checking or savings account and a credit line are the same thing. Just because you can use your credit card to buy something does not mean that you can really afford the item. A credit charge card is not like writing a check. When you charge something the money to pay for it is not deducted from the bank account where you deposit your money. Credit-card buying borrows against your future income and you pay a very high rate of interest for this luxury. The system works so smoothly that it is very easy to to become deeply indebted to the credit card company.

AWARE item 7.
People often spend more than they earn. (True)

Taking the time to create a budget—and then having the wisdom and self-control to live within it—can keep you out of financial trouble. Budgeting lets you control your money, rather than face money problems that spiral out of control. Creating a budget means actively deciding ahead of time what to spend money on, so expenses do not mount up. Setting a budget takes time. But people generally find it's time well spent.

Items commonly found in a couple's budget include the following:

- **Income**
  Husband's take-home pay
  Wife's take-home pay
  Interest earned on savings

- **Fixed expenses**
  Rent or mortgage loan payments
  Bank loan (automobile)
  Utilities
  Telephone
  Insurance
  Furniture payments
  Savings

- **Day-to-Day Expenses**
  Food
  Clothing
  Entertainment
  Personal care
  Gas, oil, insurance, and car maintenance
  Charitable contributions
  Other items

AWARE item 8.
Creating a budget can keep you out of financial struggles. (True)

A big part of the budgeting process is distinguishing between what you want and what you need. People regularly confuse wants and needs. You may *need* a car: a reliable old clunker to get you from Point A to Point B. But you may *want* a Lexus. Confusing wants and needs on a car can easily cost you $40,000.

A good way to begin creating a budget is to keep track of everything you spend money on for a given week and month. You may be surprised once you put down on paper how much you are spending. Those movie rentals and sodas add up fast.

Once you've set up a budget, sticking to it can be difficult. You will need to eliminate impulse buying and practice being disciplined with your money. In your budget you'll include a fixed amount each month for items such as gifts and entertainment. Having a definite figure in mind helps you avoid spending more than you can afford. And there's nothing quite as good as the feeling that you are in control of your money.

AWARE item 9.
People often have a difficult time creating a budget and sticking to it. (True)

Savings: It's Not What You Earn, It's What You Keep

> *Beware of little expenses, a small leak will sink a great ship.*
> — BENJAMIN FRANKLIN

Most students reading this book have not yet had the opportunity to hold a steady job for any length of time. But many of you have had part-time jobs. You may also have earned income through babysitting or yardwork or whatever. So, do this exercise: Estimate the total amount of money that you have received this year, including gifts or money from your parents. This will take a bit of time to do, and you won't be perfectly accurate. Simply make a good guess.

Now, how much of that total have you saved? Look at your savings account balance. If you're like most people, it is probably a very small percentage of the money that has gone through your hands. And most families are not much different from you. After taxes and monthly bills, most families have very little money to save or invest.

Fortunately, it does not take a lot of money to benefit from the magic of compound interest. *Compound interest* is the interest one makes on savings: it includes both the interest you earn on the money you put in savings *and* the interest you earn on the interest those savings earn. Compounding pays you for doing nothing but keeping your money invested in a relatively safe, reliable place. Figure 11-2 shows how small amounts can grow into real dollars, and that it's never too soon to start.

Figure 11-2.

The Power of Compounding

No. 1—If you invest the money used to purchase your afternoon soft drink:
$.50/day @ 5 days/week = $10.00 month

	10 yrs.	20 yrs.	30 yrs.	40 yrs.	50 yrs.	60 yrs.	70 yrs.
5%	$1,559	$4,127	$ 8,357	$ 15,323	$ 26,797	$ 45,695	$ 76,820
10%	$2,065	$7,656	$22,793	$ 63,767	$174,687	$474,952	$1,287,781

No. 2—If you save $1 a day
$1/day for 30 days = $30 month

Yrs.	5%	10%
10	$ 4,677	$ 6,195
20	12,381	22,968
30	25,071	68,379
40	45,969	191,301
50	80,391	524,061
60	137,085	1,424,856
70	230,460	3,863,340

Time is on your side when it comes to saving for the future. If you begin saving a little bit of money each month when you are young and continue doing this throughout your life, your savings will grow into an astonishing amount.

If the future seems too far away, there are very important immediate reasons for getting in the habit of saving. One is to put aside enough money to pay for a college education, which generally translates into a higher income throughout your life or to have enough money to buy a car. Many financial advisors recommend that a person create an emergency fund with enough money in it to support them without any other income for at least four to six months. A serious accident, or loss of a job can quickly put you into debt.

Advantages and Disadvantages of Credit Cards

Having a credit card has a number of advantages. Credit cards are convenient, and they simplify many purchases because they are accepted at many places around the world. They also provide a record of purchases, which can be helpful. If you're short of money at the time, or need to make a major purchase and don't want to carry a lot of cash, a credit card comes in handy. Finally, credit cards are useful for unexpected expenses such as emergency medical services, automobile repairs, or a plane ticket home.

Credit cards can lead to loss of money because of finance charges. If you do not pay the entire bill each month, the credit card company adds a finance charge, which is the amount of money the lender charges you for the use of the borrowed funds. The interest rate charged by many credit card companies is very high.

The biggest problem with credit cards is that they make spending so easy that we are tempted to overspend. Paying a small minimum fee each month may seem a lot easier than paying the full price to purchase something. But we can soon find ourselves in over our heads. First we need a new jacket, then a new pair of shoes, then we think about a used car. The list is endless, the bills mount up, and debt becomes a real problem. If we don't pay off the bill in full each month—and most people don't—we quickly see more finance charges. It becomes a vicious cycle.

A financial counselor came to our contemporary family relationships class recently and spent much of his time discussing the dangers of credit cards. At one point he said to the class, "Let me give you an example of how this all works against you. Say you've just graduated from college. You worked hard, you lived cheaply and didn't have anything nice or anything new all through college. You want to reward yourself a bit."

Most class members nodded in agreement. This sounded a lot like many of their lives. "Well, say you go over to the electronics store and pick out a really good stereo system: receiver, tape deck, speakers and CD player. You plan to have this system a long time, so you get a good one. The bill comes to almost $2,000. You put it all on your credit card.

"Not long after this, you get your first statement with the $2,000 on it. The minimum payment doesn't look so bad at all. You'd like to pay it off more quickly, but you haven't got a really great-paying job yet. You don't make much more than the minimum wage, even though you're now a college graduate. So, you send the minimum payment to the credit card company each month."

"Do you have any idea how long it will take you to pay off that $2,000 making a minimum payment each month? The interest rate is a pretty common 19.8 percent."

Class members looked very thoughtful and one hazarded what seemed like a reasonable guess: "Two or three years?"

"Nope," the financial counselor said. "Try again."

"Five years!" another student blurted out. Some class members hooted. That seemed like an unreasonably long period of time for a stereo.

"Nope. It will take you 32 years to pay off your stereo at this rate. You will be locked into the credit card company for 32 years. And, you'll end up paying more than $12,000 for a stereo system that after 32 years will have absolutely no market value at all. In fact, after that long, the stereo system will be obsolete."

Class members looked shocked. It is a good reminder of why it is important to pay loans off as quickly as possible.

Debit Cards: A New Kind of Plastic

A relatively new development is the so-called debit card. It has many of the advantages of a credit card, and fewer drawbacks. A debit card looks like a credit card, but it is tied to your checking account, not to a line of credit. If you're caught short without cash or need to purchase something at a place that will not accept a personal check, you can use the debit card. The money to pay for the transaction is deducted from your checking account, even though the paperwork looks much like that for a credit card transaction.

For emergencies, your debit card can be tied into an overdraft account honored by your financial institution. If you need more money than you have in your checking account, you can simply call the financial institution and ask them to transfer funds from the overdraft account into your checking account to cover the emergency. Debit cards are useful because they offer the convenience of a credit card, but because they are tied to your checking account, it is more difficult to lose control of your spending.

Establishing Good Credit

One irony of establishing good credit is that for a lender to grant you credit, the company wants proof that you have a good credit history. This can make it difficult for those just starting out to get credit. But having no established credit history is better than having bad credit. You can prove that you have the ability to manage credit by establishing both a checking and savings account. Avoid overdrafts ("bounced checks") on the checking account and try to maintain a minimum balance in the savings account. Maintaining good credit will make it easier to get loans in the future, for example, a loan for a new house.

AWARE item 10.
Establishing a good credit history is very important for your financial future. (True)

Now that you have completed reading this material on financial decisions, go back to the beginning of the chapter and answer the questions on the AWARE quiz on "Financial Issues" again. Check your improvement.

Values, Beliefs and Behaviors

> " Keep your eye on your heroes, Not on your zeros. "
>
> ROBERT H. SCHULER,
> RELIGIOUS LEADER

Aware Quiz

Do You Live by Your Values?

Circle True or False

1 I make my own decisions, without being influenced by my family, church, or my peers.　　T or F

2 The decisions I make are often based on how positive I feel about myself.　　T or F

3 You will tend to repeat the past, good or bad, unless you consciously try to do things differently.　　T or F

4 It is okay to change my mind about my values and goals.　　T or F

5 My values and beliefs effect the decisions I make in my daily life.　　T or F

6 All people have similar spiritual beliefs.　　T or F

7 Adolescents who feel religion is important are less likely to engage in unhealthy behaviors such as smoking or drinking.　　T or F

8 The quality of one's family effects whether adolescents share the spiritual beliefs of their parents.　　T or F

9 People who succeed are not necessarily the smartest, but they are the most motivated.　　T or F

10 Having a mentor is helpful in reaching your goals.　　T or F

*Please complete the QUIZ
before reading the chapter.*

Choices

Adolescence or young adulthood is generally the time when you develop a sense of independence and choose your own values and beliefs about a variety of different issues. As a young child, your family seems like your whole world and what your family does appears to be the *only* way to live. As you grow up, however, countless other influences come into play in your life. You quickly learn that your family's approach to living is just one of many possible paths. As you grow older you also begin to value your independence and to strive to make decisions about your life from your own personal perspective.

Influences on Your Decisions

But we don't make decisions about our life in a vacuum, even as adults. An individual cannot be understood apart from the context in which he or she grows up. Family, friends, classmates, and our own desires all affect the choices we make.

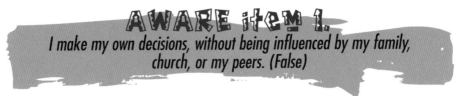

AWARE iteM 1.
I make my own decisions, without being influenced by my family, church, or my peers. (False)

Peer pressure, the need to be accepted by people in your age group, is significant at any age. Children, adolescents, and adults, commonly do what their peers are doing. Peer pressure can lead people to do things they might otherwise not do in order to gain acceptance and approval from others.

Parental expectations are also important for young people. Growing up in your family you become aware of what your parents and other family members expect from you. You may not always be consciously aware of these expectations because they become so much a part of your own value system. For example, many parents value education and assume that their children will continue their schooling after they graduate from high school. Their children make plans for college but may never have independently made the decision to attend. Family expectations often have a positive influence on the family members' choices you make, but if parental expectations are too strict or inflexible, young people may rebel.

In a comprehensive study of more than 90,000 students, researchers found that adolescents whose parents had high expectations for school performance were relatively protected against emotional distress. "Emotional distress" included self-reports of depression, loneliness, fear, sadness, moodiness, and poor appetite. Why would this be so? One explanation is that having well-defined goals in life can bring people comfort. The goal of good performance in school is socially accepted and respected, and identifying with an important purpose in life can be comforting. The key, of course, is not overdoing a good thing. Young people can become overburdened and unhappy in the face of impossibly high expectations that make failure more likely.

Besides peers and parents, *self-image* can also be a very significant influence on the choices we make. Your self-image—how you think of yourself—is developed and reinforced by how others treat you and react to you. Self-image is also a result of our thoughts. Thinking about something positive helps build your self image. Self-image is important. Young people who have negative self-images may find it difficult to make decisions, or may make decisions that may jeopardize their health. One young man told us, "My father was always putting me down. It went on and on and on. He told me I was stupid so many times I finally decided, 'Forget him! I'll prove that he's right!' The young man began drinking and taking other drugs in an effort to mask the anger he felt toward his father—and as a way of punishing his father. The angry young man's plan backfired, of course, and resulted in addiction and a downward spiral into despair.

AWARE item 2.
The decisions I make are often based on how positive I feel about myself. (True)

Your Past Is Not Your Future

Although we are what we are partially because of the experiences we have had in the past, our past does not have to be our future. We can choose to build on the good experiences which have given us confidence or made us feel valued and to forget the negative experiences. You don't drive down the road constantly looking in the rearview mirror. You look where you're going not where you've been.

AWARE item 3.
You will tend to repeat the past, good or bad, unless you consciously try to do things differently. (True)

"You can clutch the past so tightly to your chest that it leaves your arms too full to embrace the present."
—JAN GLIDEWELL

What You Were Is Not What You Are

We all change. Just as our bodies change and outgrow old clothes, our beliefs, values, goals, and preferences can change as well. Adolescence is a time of many changes. It is a time for discovering who you are and what your identity is. It is completely normal to change your mind about many issues.

AWARE item 4.
It is okay to change my mind about my values and goals. (True)

It is also important to realize, with the increasing independence you have in decision making, that some of the decisions which you make are difficult to change. For example, choosing to smoke, drink, use other drugs, have unprotected sex, or engage in criminal behaviors are choices that can have lifetime consequences. One woman tells this story about her choices:

> I started smoking cigarettes when I was 13 or 14. At first I hated them, but I thought they made me look more mature. And the group of kids I ran with all were trying them out, so it seemed okay at the time.
>
> About the same time I started drinking sometimes. I liked the warm, fuzzy feeling alcohol gave me. I was a high-energy, kind of high-strung young girl, and it calmed me down. It took the edge off me. I continued smoking and drinking through college even though I was trained as a biologist and knew what all this was doing to my body.
>
> I quit drinking after it got me in trouble at work, and I'm still trying to stop smoking.

Values and Beliefs

A *value* is something that is important to us. A *belief* is something that we hold to be true. Value refers to the worth or importance you assign to a certain belief, activity, or event. We do not create our values and beliefs in a vacuum. They are influenced by those around us: people in our home, school, place of worship, and society in general all influence our thinking in regard to values and beliefs. For example, if family members and friends value going to church or

223

synagogue and believe in the teachings of the church or synagogue, we most likely will accept those values and beliefs as our own.

Interconnected Values, Beliefs, and Behaviors

Our actions—behaviors—often express our values and goals. Similarly, our beliefs and values often determine our behaviors. People usually act in ways that are consistent with their values. For example, a person who tells lies is most likely not a person who values honesty. Likewise, a person who does not value honesty is likely to be someone who cannot be trusted to tell the truth.

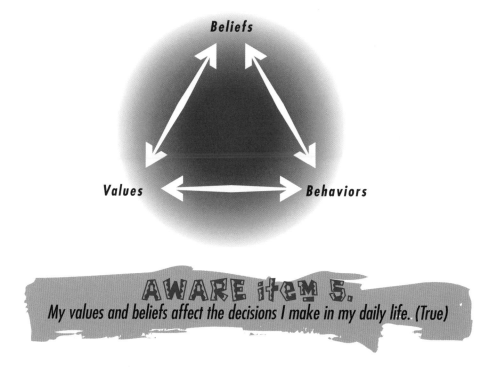

AWARE item 5.
My values and beliefs affect the decisions I make in my daily life. (True)

Role of Spiritual or Religious Beliefs

Spiritual or religious beliefs can provide a base for an individual's values and behaviors. Some people have very defined beliefs related to their spirituality; others do not. There are many different systems of belief or faith throughout the world. Even within the same religious group, individuals often differ quite a bit in their beliefs and in the way they express those beliefs.

AWARE item 6.
All people have similar spiritual beliefs. (False)

Because spiritual beliefs vary so much, it can be difficult to find others with beliefs identical to our own. In fact, because beliefs are so personal, it is quite common for husbands and wives to have different views, and for children to have different views than their parents and grandparents.

These differences can be seen as a problem or a strength, depending on your personal values. If you choose to see uniqueness as important and interesting, then different spiritual or religious beliefs in a relationship or a family do not necessarily have to be a source of problems. "Variety is the spice of life," it has been said many times.

Differing beliefs are just one aspect of our uniqueness as human beings: they need not be a barrier to getting to know others but can be a source of interest and attraction. If all of us in the world were the same, it would get pretty boring. We wouldn't have much to talk about because we would know what the other person was going to say before he or she said it.

Religious groups play an important role in promoting healthy behaviors. The National Longitudinal Study of Adolescent Health (Benson, 1995) found that adolescents who report religion and prayer as important in their lives, are less likely than other adolescents to smoke cigarettes, drink alcohol, or use marijuana and are more likely to delay sexual activity until they are older.

AWARE item 7.

Adolescents who feel religion is important are less likely to engage in unhealthy behaviors such as smoking or drinking. (True)

This same study found evidence that family worship has a powerful influence on an adolescent's spiritual beliefs if parent and child have a quality relationship. Young people tend to accept the religious beliefs and values of their parents if the relationship between parent and adolescent is a good one. Parents who use religion to control their adolescent children often find that they get the opposite result: the adolescent may reject the parents' religious beliefs altogether.

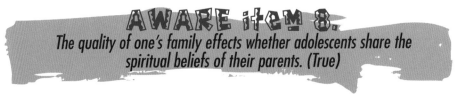

AWARE item 8.
The quality of one's family effects whether adolescents share the spiritual beliefs of their parents. (True)

Identifying Your Own Values

Spiritual or religious beliefs give life meaning, hope, and direction for many people. Believing in something beyond the material world gives many people a sense of purpose in life. When used in positive ways, spiritual or religious beliefs can enhance our relationships with others.

Determining what your personal values are can help you understand more about yourself and your behaviors. It's also an important step in forming lasting relationship with others. The questionnaire in Box 12-1 is designed to help you identify what you consider important in life. Rank the items, and then follow the scoring instructions to interpret the results.

Box 12-1.

Insights into Your Values

Rank the following characteristics in terms of their value or importance to you. Assign a number 7 to the item that is the *most* important to you and a number 1 to the item that is the least important within each of the three groups.

Group 1: Rank from 7 (most important) to 1 (least important):

a. _____ Education

b _____ Spending time with my family

c. _____ Having fun

d. _____ Wanting to be seen as a winner

e. _____ Meeting people

f. _____ Caring about others

g. _____ Having a lot of money

Group 2: Rank from 7 (most important) to 1 (least important):

h. _____ Having people see me as powerful

i. _____ Being physically attractive (nice clothes, hair, physique, etc.)

j. _____ Getting along with parents

k. _____ Spending time with friends

l. _____ Being happy

m. _____ Understanding others

n. _____ Having a successful career

Group 3: Rank from 7 (most important) to 1 (least important):

o. _____ Being liked by others

p. _____ Making a good impression on others

q. _____ Feeling understood by my family

r. _____ Being a good listener

s. _____ Driving a nice car

t. _____ Doing what I want

u. _____ Developing a specific talent or skill (a sport, writing, musical instrument, public speaking, etc.)

Scoring of "Insight into Your Values"

1. Add your numbers for items g, i, and s. $(g + i + s = $ _____ $)$.

2. Add your numbers for items c, l, and t. $(c + l + t = $ _____ $)$.

3. Add your numbers for items f, m, and r. $(f + m + r = $ _____ $)$.

4. Add your numbers for items a, n, and u. $(a + n + u = $ _____ $)$.

5. Add your numbers for items d, h, and p. $(d + h + p = $ _____ $)$.

6. Add your numbers for items e, k, and o. $(e + k + o = $ _____ $)$.

7. Add your numbers for items b, j, and q. $(b + j + q = $ _____ $)$.

Profile of Your Value Priorities

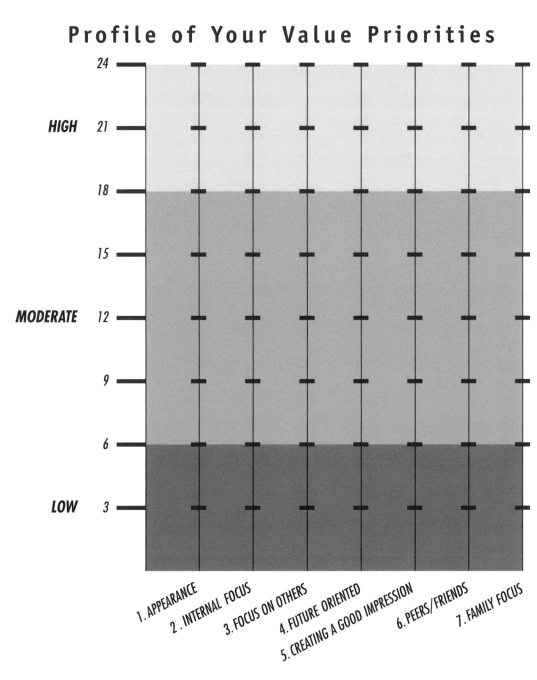

After you have computed your scores on the previous page for each area, plot them onto the chart. Then connect the scores with a line.

Interpretation of "Insights into Your Values"

You calculated seven scores ranging from 3 to 21. The section above the scores (numbered 1–7) correlates with seven general areas to which people attach value. Your highest score represents the area you regard as having the most importance, and your lowest score represents what you value the least. Generally, a score between 3 and 9 in any area is low; between 9 and 18 is moderate; and between 18 and 21 is high.

1. Appearance and material things (items g, i, and s)

Having a lot of money

Physical appearance (clothing, hair, physique, etc.)

Driving a nice car

A high score in this area indicates that you place a high value on external or material things, such as having nice clothing and valuable possessions.

2. Internal focus (items c, l, and t)

Having fun

Being happy

Doing what I want

A high score in this area indicates that your primary focus is on yourself—having fun and perhaps having your feelings acknowledged.

3. Focus on others (items f, m, and r)

Caring about others

Understanding others

Being a good listener

A high score in this area indicates that you are very responsive to others' needs, you value personal relationships, and generally look for the good in others.

4. Future oriented (items a, n, and u)

Education

A "successful" career

Developing a specific talent (a sport, writing, musical instrument, public speaking, etc).

A high score in this area indicates that you are very future and goal-oriented. You tend to focus on activities that teach skills or self-improvement.

5. Creating a good impression (items d, h, and p)

Wanting to be seen as a winner

Having people see me as powerful

Making a good impression on others

A high score in this area indicates that you strive for accomplishment, may be competitive, and value recognition for your contributions.

6. Peers/friends (items e, k, and o)

Meeting people

Spending time with friends

Being liked by others

A high score in this area indicates that you like to interact with many people and that you value social situations and the approval of others.

7. Family focus (items b, j, and q)

Spending time with my family

Getting along with parents

Feeling understood by my parents/family

A high score in this area indicates that you understand the value of your family and also value having quality relationships with your parents and family.

Reaching Goals

Our values and beliefs are important because they are the foundation from which we make decisions in our lives and develop goals for ourselves. Goals are broad statements of what we want to achieve. There is no easy way to reach—and let alone exceed all of our goals. It takes time and energy to achieve any goal. A good way to achieve goals is to set objectives—short-range actions—that will lead to those goals. Ask yourself, "Is what I am doing right now bringing me closer to reaching my goals?"

Success in life—however one may define it—is achieved by focusing on what you believe is important and acting in ways that move you closer to these goals. Sometimes the smartest people in the world do not reach their goals because they fail to commit energy and enthusiasm to the task. But the rest of us—seemingly "ordinary people"—often become quite successful because we know how to work at it.

Commitment and motivation are essential in healthy human relationships. In fact, commitment is essential in achieving any important goal. According to John H. Mennear:

> The important thing is to stick to it. As American journalist Jacob A. Riis once said: "When nothing seems to help, I go and look at the stonecutter hammering away at his rock, perhaps a hundred times without as much as a crack showing in it. Yet, at the hundred and first blow it will split in two, and I know it was not that last blow that did it, but all that had gone before."

Mentors

A mentor, according to the dictionary, is "a wise and trusted counselor or teacher." Because "we are all teachers and we are all learners," there are countless mentors in the world who can capably guide us through life's ups and downs. A mentor can simply be a person who is farther down the road than you are—someone who has achieved what you would like to achieve. It can be a neighbor, a relative, a friend of your family or someone you have observed that you admire.

In our classes we encourage our students to go out and find mentors. Many people are eager to play the mentor role. "I am very happy to share my experiences in life with younger people," one woman told us. "Rather than have them waste a whole lot of time reinventing the wheel, I can help them reach their goals without all the frustrations I felt." Study others whom you like and admire. We all have so much to learn from each other.

Find mentors for your life, and ask them how they got where they are:

- What strategies did they use?
- How do they organize their life?
- What books did they read?
- What people did they work with?
- What life experiences did they have?
- How did they do it?

232

You will be surprised how many people will be only too happy to answer all your questions and give you really good ideas for reaching your goals.

AWARE item 10.
Having a mentor is helpful in reaching your goals. (True)

Just Do It!

In life a person can play a passive role or an active one. If you wish to achieve your goals, we believe it is important to play an active role. Marva Collins says it quite well: "Success doesn't come to you, you go to it." If one of your goals in life is financial well-being, you will have to work to achieve it. If you seek positive, loving relationships with your partner, your family, and your friends, you will have to learn about healthy relationships and conscientiously work to create them. If you want to be of service to God and to humankind, you will have to painstakingly develop skills that will make a difference in the world.

You can have the world's greatest car in your garage, but unless you start it up, it will not take you anywhere. The best way to achieve your dreams, to access your potential, is to Just Do It! Set a goal and follow through with it. The philosopher and psychologist Williams said, "There's nothing as fatiguing as holding on to an uncompleted task." Taking "baby" steps toward your goals may be tiring at first, but you will find it energizing once you have started and are into it.

For thousands of years the Chinese have believed that "the journey of a thousand miles begins with a single step." Creating loving relationships and a meaningful way of living for ourselves is a wonderful, lifelong journey. Today is a perfect day to begin.

❧

How about going back now and seeing if your score on the AWARE quiz on the "Values, Beliefs, and Behaviors" scale has improved?

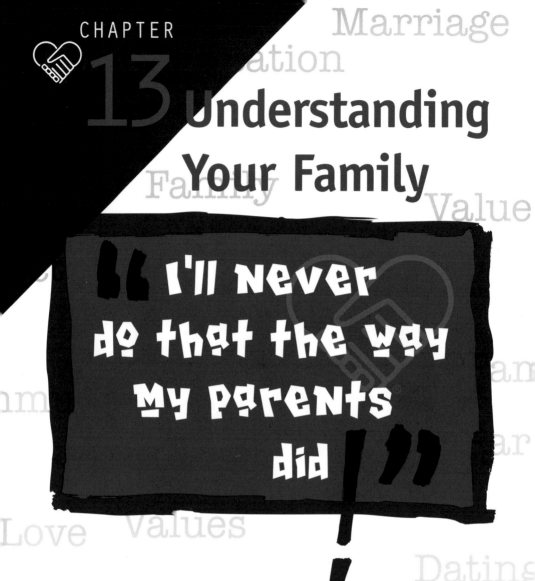

Understanding Your Family

"I'll never do that the way my parents did"

Aware Quiz: Family Strengths

Circle the response that best describes your family.

Family Closeness

1 *How close do you feel to other family members?*

1	2	3	4
Not very close	Generally close	Very close	Extremely close

2 *How often does your family spend free time together?*

1	2	3	4
Seldom	Sometimes	Often	Very often

3 *How does your family balance separateness and togetherness?*

1	2	3	4
Mainly separate	More separate than together	More together than separate	Mainly together

4 *How independent of or dependent on the family are family members?*

1	2	3	4
Very independent	More independent than dependent	More dependent than independent	Very dependent

5 *Answer either Part a or Part b:*

a. *For families with two parents, how close are the husband and the wife?*

1	2	3	4
Not very close	Generally close	Very close	Extremely close

b. *For families with single parents, how close is your parent to the children?*

1	2	3	4
Not very close	Generally close	Very close	Extremely close

Add your responses to these questions to get a total Closeness score.

FAMILY CLOSENESS SCORE:

Circle the response that best describes your family.

Family Flexibility

1 *What kind of leadership is there in your family?*

1	2	3	4
One person usually leads	Leadership is sometimes shared	Leadership is generally shared	No Clear leader

2 *How often do family members do the same things (roles) around the house?*

1	2	3	4
Always	Often	Sometimes	Seldom

3 *What are the rules (written or unwritten) like in your family?*

1	2	3	4
Rules very clear and very stable	Rules clear and generally stable	Rules clear and flexible	Rules not clear and change often

4 *How is discipline of the children handled?*

1	2	3	4
Very strict	Somewhat democratic	Democratic	Very lenient

5 *How open is your family to making changes when they are necessary?*

1	2	3	4
Seldom open	Somewhat open	Generally open	Very open

Add your responses to these questions to get a total Flexibility score.

FAMILY FLEXIBILITY SCORE:

Figure 13-1.

Family Map For Graphing Your Family

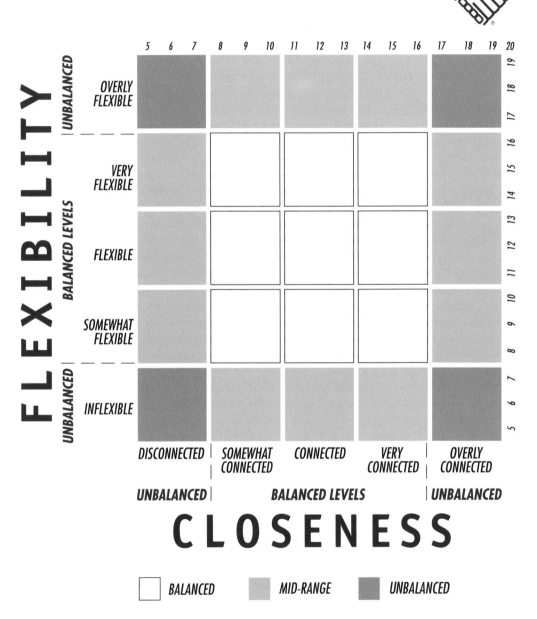

Directions For Locating Your Family On The Family Map

Along the bottom of the Family Map is the closeness scale; on the left side is the flexibility scale. *Find your score on each of the scales on the previous page, and plot a point where the two scores meet.*

You will note that for each of the two scales and the Family Map, closeness and flexibility are broken down into five levels. Write down the names of the closeness and flexibility levels that coincide with your scores. After you have read this chapter, you can return to this quiz and interpret what your scores mean.

"I'll Never Do That the Way My Parents Did!"

If you are like most teenagers today, you have often thought about how you would do things differently from your parents. As you have grown and made more of your own decisions, you have probably been in situations where you have told yourself you would not act in the same way your parents did. Everyone experiences these feelings. Parents and their young-adult children inevitably disagree on occasion.

Despite your promise to do things differently than your parents, you are more influenced by your parents than you may be aware. You have internalized many of your beliefs and ideas about yourself and the world from your parents. In other words, these ideas and beliefs have become so much a part of you that you are not even aware of them or where they came from. This is why it may be easier for you to recognize some of the problems that your friends are going through with their families than to see what is happening in your own family.

Your parents and family have a very powerful impact on your life and the way you see the world. Your feelings and ideas are closely involved with those of your parents. It can be difficult to step outside of your family and it's way of operating to look objectively at things. It's like the expression: "A fish doesn't know it's in water." In some ways, we all grow up in different oceans—oceans containing many creatures and elements to which we have grown accustomed.

Family Influences on Our Actions and Attitudes

We know that the family in which we grow up (our family-of-origin) plays a big part in shaping how we view the world. What happens, then, when two people marry and create their own unique family? Often, they try to recreate the family environment in which they grew up—both the positives and the negatives. And because each partner comes from a unique family, there is often conflict over how to build this new family. Each partner finds it difficult to see the world from the other's perspective. Therefore, the better we understand our family-of-origin, the more successful we will be in determining what we want to bring from our family-of-origin into our adult life and future relationships—and what we want to leave behind.

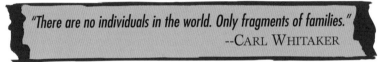

"There are no individuals in the world. Only fragments of families."
--CARL WHITAKER

The late Carl Whitaker was a world renowned family therapist at the University of Wisconsin-Madison. Dr. Whitaker believed that human beings live so closely in families that it is probably impossible to understand an individual without seeing how that individual fits into her or his family. We are like pieces of a puzzle, and we cannot see and understand the whole picture of the family until we fit the individual pieces together.

Early treatment programs for troubled children and young people often removed the troubled individual from the family and placed her or him in a treatment center. However, the clinicians often found that the child would get better at the treatment center, but soon after returning home would exhibit the same problem behaviors as before. This led to the belief that problem behaviors do not arise only from *within the child* but are related to problems *within the family*. This is one of the fundamental beliefs of what today is called family systems theory.

To understand an individual's behavior today we need to look at the family and the broader culture. Guided by an approach called the family ecological perspective, it is important not only to understand a family's dynamics but also to understand the larger systems in which the family lives: the extended family, their peers, the neighborhood, the schools, the church or synagogue, and the community as a whole.

All these larger systems influence how individuals and families behave, and families also exert influence on these greater systems.

Three Qualities That Determine a Family's Dynamics

Dr. David Olson and his colleagues at the University of Minnesota, guided by family systems theory, have chosen to focus their efforts on relationships within the family. They developed a way to understand one's family by representing the dynamics of family relationships in terms of three qualities: **closeness, flexibility** and **communication.** These qualities are represented on something called the Family Map (it's formal name is the Family Circumplex Model) which was shown in Figure 13-1. Family systems theory applies equally to couples who are simply families without children. Each of these three qualities (also termed "dimensions") is explained in this chapter.

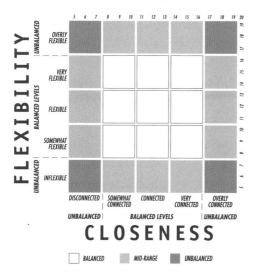

Family Closeness

Closeness is the *emotional closeness you feel toward another person*—in this context to members of your family. You might call it togetherness. The Family Map breaks down the closeness into five levels (degrees of togetherness): *Disconnected, Somewhat Connected, Connected, Very Connected and Overly Connected.*

Finding a balance between **separateness** and **togetherness** is the key to healthy family closeness. Although being *Disconnected*, (too much separateness) or *Overly Connected* (too much togetherness) can be appropriate at times, relationships that always operate at these extremes can be unhealthy. It is normal for families to shift back and forth between togetherness and separateness depending on what is happening in the family. But families that get locked into an extreme level of closeness (or lack of it) tend to have more problems.

Figure 13-2 shows the five levels of family closeness. Finding the balance between separateness and togetherness is not necessarily easy, and families often lose their balance. Family therapists and family educators commonly believe that the three middle positions in Figure 13-2 work best for families. In a *Connected family system*, the balance between separateness and togetherness is about equal. Family members feel good about the amount of time they spend together and how close they feel to each other; but there is also adequate time and encouragement for individuals to pursue outside interests—career, community service, hobbies, and other activities. Balance, of course, is difficult to achieve.

Many families teeter up and down a bit. Look at the *Somewhat Connected system* in Figure 13-2 to see a family relationship that leans a bit more toward separateness, then look at the *Very Connected system* which leans a bit toward the togetherness side. All three of these positions produce generally workable family relationships.

Figure 13-2.

Five Levels of Family Closeness: Balancing Separateness and Togetherness

DISCONNECTED SYSTEM	SEPARATENESS VS. TOGETHERNESS	UNBALANCED HIGH SEPARATENESS
SOMEWHAT CONNECTED SYSTEM	SEPARATENESS VS. TOGETHERNESS	BALANCED MORE SEPARATENESS THAN TOGETHERNESS
CONNECTED SYSTEM	SEPARATENESS VS. TOGETHERNESS	BALANCED EQUAL SEPARATENESS AND TOGETHERNESS
VERY CONNECTED SYSTEM	SEPARATENESS VS. TOGETHERNESS	BALANCED MORE TOGETHERNESS THAN SEPARATENESS
OVERLY CONNECTED SYSTEM	SEPARATENESS VS. TOGETHERNESS	UNBALANCED VERY HIGH TOGETHERNESS

241

Take a look at Table 13-1 for another way of thinking about family closeness and the balance between separateness and togetherness. The left-hand column of the table lists the six main characteristics of family closeness: *separateness-togetherness, I-We balance, closeness, loyalty, activities and dependence-independence*. Across the top of Table 13-1 are the five levels of family closeness: *Disconnected, Somewhat Connected, Connected, Very Connected, and Overly Connected*. Reading down the column under a specific family closeness level gives a clear picture of the characteristics of that level.

Table 13-1.

Defining the Levels of Family Closeness

CHARACTERISTIC	DISCONNECTED (Unbalanced)	SOMEWHAT CONNECTED (Balanced)	CONNECTED (Balanced)	VERY CONNECTED (Balanced)	OVERLY CONNECTED (Unbalanced)
SEPARATENESS-TOGETHERNESS	High separateness	More Separateness than togetherness	A balance of separateness and togetherness	More togetherness than separateness	Very high togetherness
I-WE BALANCE	Primarily I	More I than We	A Balance of I and We	More We than I	Primarily We
CLOSENESS	Little closeness	Low to moderate closeness	Moderate closeness	Moderate to high closeness	Very high closeness
LOYALTY	Lack of loyalty	Some loyalty	Moderate loyalty	Considerable loyalty	High loyalty
ACTIVITIES	Mainly separate	More separate than shared	Some separate some shared	More shared than separate	Mainly shared
DEPENDENCE-INDEPENDENCE	High Independence	More independence than dependence	Interdependence	More dependence than independence	High dependence

Extreme Togetherness and Extreme Separateness. Having a very low or a very high level of family closeness can eventually lead to problems. When a family is **disconnected**—when family members are not very close to one another—family members tend to focus only on themselves and they lack a sense of loyalty to the family. They often show little interest or concern for one another's well-being. Family members feel that they cannot count on their family to give them support if they need it. Under stress or in a crisis, a disconnected family cannot work together to help its members, and the family can splinter apart.

Separateness Poem (Extreme Separateness)

The poem, by psychotherapist Fritz Perls, describes extreme separateness very well. When each person focuses mainly on themselves, it is hard to develop a close relationship.

> I do my thing and you do your thing.
> I am not in this world to live up to your expectations.
> And you are not in this world to live up to mine.
> You are you, and I am I.
> And if by chance we meet, it's beautiful.
> If not, it can't be helped.
>
> Perls, F. (1969). Gestalt therapy verbatim (p.4). Lafayette, CA Real People Press.

Togetherness Poem (Extreme Togetherness)

On the other hand, families that have an extreme amount of emotional closeness over a long period of time are not healthy either. Family members in an **overly connected family** are very dependent on one another and little private space or time is usually permitted. The family is viewed as much more important than the individual, and it is often difficult for overly connected families to *let go* of another family member during normal life transitions, such as going off to college. Judy Altura has described this type of family poetically:

> We do everything together.
> I am here to meet all your needs and expectations.
> And you are here to meet mine.
> We had to meet, and it was beautiful.
> I can't imagine it turning out any other way.
>
> Altura, J. (1974), Poem. In J. Gillies, My needs, your needs. New York: Doubleday.

Balancing Separateness & Togetherness.

Families with a good balance between separateness and togetherness enjoy being together, but also allow for individuality and time apart from family members. A balanced family on togetherness is committed to the family members, but they are also able to "do their own thing." Individual members are able to be both independent from and connected to their family.

The way our families-of-origin operated in terms of closeness is important because we will tend to automatically operate in the same way, unless we make very deliberate attempts to change that learned pattern. For example, in a dating-type relationship, let's pretend that a woman came from an *Overly Connected* family where birthdays were very important and recognized by all family members. In fact, birthdays were a big deal and a time to celebrate a person's life. Now this woman is dating a man whose family was *Disconnected*. In his family, birthdays were hardly even recognized. When the woman has her birthday, the man may not acknowledge her in the way she is used to being treated on her "special day". Likewise, if she makes a big deal of his birthday, he may feel awkward.

Extreme togetherness is especially common in the early stages of a couple's relationship. There is such a powerful emotional/physical attraction between the two that they may feel empty, isolated and incomplete when they are away from each other. But couples typically do not feel "love-sick" for long. Healthy relationships evolve over time into a workable balance of separateness and togetherness.

We have a third poem to present to you that describes this delicate, wonderful balance between separateness and togetherness. It is by a philosopher, Kahlil Gibran:

On Marriage

Love one another, but make not a bond of love;
Let it rather be a moving sea between the shores of your souls.
Fill each other's cup, but drink not from the same cup.
Give one another of your bread, but eat not from the same loaf.
Sing and dance together and be joyous,
But let each one of you be alone,
Even as the strings of a flute are alone
Though they quiver with the same music
Give your hearts, but not into each other's keeping.
For only the hand of Life can contain your hearts.
And stand together yet not too near together;
For the pillars of the temple stand apart,
And the oak tree and the cypress grow
Not in each other's shadow.
But let there be space in your togetherness,
And let the winds of the heavens dance between you.

Gibran, K (1923/1976). The Prophet (pp. 16-17). New York: Knopf.

The relationship Gibran describes is an ideal. In the real world of loving relationships, few find this perfect balance with their partner. It is a noble goal, but one that is difficult to achieve and maintain for a long period of time. It is also important to note that in intimate relationships, people can experience and even enjoy, at least for a short time, both extremes on the togetherness-separateness continuum. Couples can remain in love with each other while also enjoying being apart for periods of time. Love is best maintained when there is a good balance of separateness and togetherness.

Family Flexibility

The second major dimension of family relationships is flexibility. **Flexibility** refers to the *openness to change that exists within a family.* It describes the amount of change that occurs, for example, in leadership, role relationships, and relationship rules. As with closeness, there are five levels of flexibility: *Inflexible, Somewhat Flexible, Flexible, Very Flexible, and Overly Flexible.*

The challenge of family flexibility is to balance *stability vs. change.* Families need a basic foundation that gives them stability, but they also need to be open to change when necessary. Ability to change is particularly important when families are under stress and need to adapt to a crisis.

Figure 13-3 shows the five levels of family flexibility. It is not easy to find the delicate balance between stability and ability to change in family life. Families often fall out of balance, becoming excessively rigid (Inflexible) or, on the other extreme, chaotic (Overly Flexible). The middle positions in Figure 13-3 seem to work best for most families. In a family system that has a good balance in the area of flexibility, family members feel good about how open they are to change but they are not so constantly open to change that they lose their sense of stability and permanence.

Figure 13-3.

INFLEXIBLE SYSTEM	STABILITY VS. CHANGE	UNBALANCED VERY LITTLE CHANGE
SOMEWHAT FLEXIBLE SYSTEM	STABILITY VS. CHANGE	BALANCED SOME CHANGE
FLEXIBLE SYSTEM	STABILITY VS. CHANGE	BALANCED MODERATE CHANGE
VERY FLEXIBLE SYSTEM	STABILITY VS. CHANGE	BALANCED CONSIDERABLE CHANGE
OVERLY FLEXIBLE SYSTEM	STABILITY VS. CHANGE	UNBALANCED A LOT OF CHANGE

Five Levels of Family Flexibility

Table 13-2 shows another way of thinking about family flexibility and the balance between stability and change, giving more information about each of the five family flexibility levels. The left-hand column of the table lists six characteristics of family flexibility: **leadership, discipline, negotiation, roles, rules, and change.**

Across the top of Table 13-2 are the five levels of family flexibility. Studying the descriptive phrases under each of the family flexibility levels increases our understanding of the characteristics of each of the five levels of family flexibility.

Table 13-2.

Defining the Levels of Family Flexibility

	INFLEXIBLE	SOMEWHAT FLEXIBLE	FLEXIBLE	VERY FLEXIBLE	OVERLY FLEXIBLE
CHARACTERISTIC	(Unbalanced)	(Balanced)	(Balanced)	(Balanced)	(Unbalanced)
LEADERSHIP	Authoritarian	Sometimes shared	Shared leadership	Often shared	Lack of leadership
DISCIPLINE	Strict Discipline	Somewhat Democratic	Democratic	Often democratic	Lenient discipline
NEGOTIATION	Limited discussion	Organized discussion	Some discussion	Open discussion	Endless discussion
ROLES	Roles very stable	Roles stable	Flexible roles	Role sharing	Dramatic role shifts
RULES	Rules very clear, stable	Rules clear and stable	Rules clear, flexible	Rules flexible and changing	Rules unclear
CHANGE	Very little change	Some change	Moderate change	Considerable change	A lot of change

Balancing Stability and Change

Families balanced on flexibility are able to maintain some stability, but are also open to change. The family system is able to change its power structure, role relationship, and relationship rules in order to adapt to situations or new developments in the family.

For example, Julie and Michael had a very balanced relationship in terms of flexibility. They had been married for 3 years, and both been working full-time when they discovered they were expecting a child. Julie and Michael had to discuss many issues such as, "Will we both continue to work full-time once the baby is born? How will we share the responsibilities of caring for our child? Will our current roles and rules change to fit our new lifestyle?" Since their marital relationship was already operating in a flexible and balanced way, they were able to function and adapt to the birth of their child in a more functional way.

Extreme Stability and Extreme Change

An *Inflexible family* may have many rules that are "written in stone." These rules typically do not change over time, and family members are rarely open to considering changes to accommodate special situations and normal life changes. Role behaviors (who does what in the family) may rarely change in inflexible families. For example, the mother may always do the shopping and meal preparation, even when it may not be convenient for her. A common issue in inflexible families is that one person in the family (usually the father or oldest man) is the decision maker, or at least always has the *final say* in family matters.

By nature, families and individuals tend to resist change, which means they naturally lean slightly toward the inflexible end of the flexibility continuum. But at the other extreme are *Overly Flexible* families, those that have so much change that they are chaotic. These families function almost completely without structure, roles, or rules. Constant or excessive change is problematic; it can be disruptive to family members and does not promote feelings of safety and reliability within the family. It is difficult for Overly Flexible families to make decisions since family members function mostly in an independent manner. When rules and roles are always changing, things often do not get done and lack of order limits the ability of these families to be productive.

Both *Inflexible* and *Overly Flexible* families lack a good balance of flexibility. Families who are more balanced between stability and change are able to grow and change over time as their individual members grow and change.

The Couple Family Map as a Relationship Map

Looking at the Couple Family Map as a relationship map, we can identify 25 types of couple and family relationships (Figure 13-4). The logic is quite simple: the dimensions of closeness and flexibility each have five levels, and 5 x 5 = 25. A marriage or a family relationship can be classified as one of these 25 types based on how the parties function in terms of closeness and flexibility. This relationship map graphically represents the relationship or system dynamics.

25 Types of Couples & Families

The 25 types of couple and family relationships can be clustered into three general types: Balanced families, Mid-range families, and Unbalanced families. *Balanced families* are those that fit into the nine central categories on the relationship map in Figure 13-4. *Mid-range families* are extreme on one dimension (for example, closeness), but balanced on the other (for example, flexibility). *Unbalanced families* are those that score at the extreme levels on both dimensions.

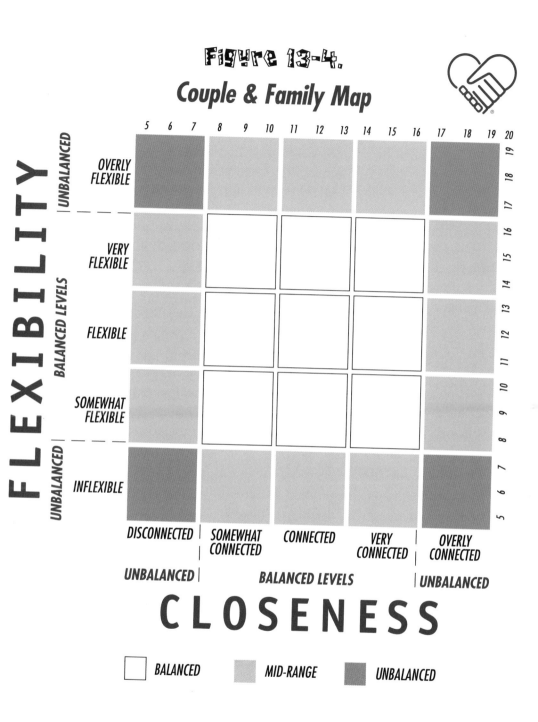

Figure 13-4.
Couple & Family Map

FLEXIBILITY

UNBALANCED — OVERLY FLEXIBLE

BALANCED LEVELS — VERY FLEXIBLE / FLEXIBLE / SOMEWHAT FLEXIBLE

UNBALANCED — INFLEXIBLE

DISCONNECTED | SOMEWHAT CONNECTED | CONNECTED | VERY CONNECTED | OVERLY CONNECTED

UNBALANCED | BALANCED LEVELS | UNBALANCED

CLOSENESS

☐ BALANCED   ▨ MID-RANGE   ▧ UNBALANCED

250

A Snapshot of Balanced Families

Families that are balanced on the closeness dimension allow their members to be both independent from and connected to the family. Families balanced on flexibility maintain some stability but are also open to change. Balanced family types can experience the extremes of the dimensions when necessary to deal with a situation, but they do not typically function at those extremes for long periods of time.

Families that have a healthy and happy relationship find a good balance between spending time together and separately. Each family member can act independently while at the same time being interdependent with other family members. Balanced families recognize the individual *selves* within the *we* of the family.

Balancing flexibility in family relationships is important as well. Change is a normal part of life and families must be open to it and willing to adapt when necessary. But families also need stability and consistency, especially in terms of discipline of the children, rules, and roles. Constant change in the family system may make family members feel insecure and unsafe.

Maintaining a balanced, healthy family system takes effort and commitment, but the rewards are worth the effort. Balanced family types are healthier and more functional than unbalanced family types.

Family Communication

Communication is the third dimension (or quality) that is important for understanding family relationships. Communication means sharing thoughts and feelings with another person. Good communication helps couples and families establish and keep balance in terms of closeness and flexibility. Couples and families that are Unbalanced (at the extremes of the closeness and/or flexibility continuums) tend to have problems communicating. Balanced families have more positive communication skills than Unbalanced families.

Family Types and Stress

To learn why some families cope well with stress and others do not, David Olson, Hamilton McCubbin, and their colleagues focused on specific family resources and also evaluated the type of family system around which families were organized. Two conclusions were very evident from their study of 1,000 families: (1) Balanced families coped better with stress than Unbalanced families and (2) Balanced families had better communication and better problem-solving skills than Unbalanced families.

Balanced families cope more effectively with stress because they tend to see problems as challenges to be dealt with rather than as signs of weakness to be avoided. The researchers looked at families across the life-span: young couples without children; families with young children; families with teenagers; and older couples. They compared stress levels and satisfaction levels among these four family groupings and found that family stress is generally highest and family satisfaction is lowest when there are adolescents in the home.

They also wanted to know why some families with adolescents coped more effectively with stress than others did. They discovered that families who coped well were headed by couples with a strong marriage relationship and good parent-adolescent communication. Although the strength of the marriage relationship was important at all stages, the strength of the marriage was especially important when adolescents were challenging parental authority and seeking their own independence.

Family Changes in Response to a Crisis

Let's see how one balanced family functions during a crisis—in this case, of the husband's (father's) heart attack. The family map in Figure 13-5 shows how the family's structure changes during this time of stress and then ultimately returns to another balanced level. Before the husband's heart attack (point A), the family is healthy and balanced. The family is *Flexible* in how it handles changes in life, and family members are *Somewhat Connected* to one another.

The father's heart attack is a tremendous shock to the family and immediately after the father is hospitalized, the family becomes Unbalanced (point B). They become both *Overly Flexible* (stunned by the heart attack, they are unable to respond in an organized and systematic manner and seem to thrash around ineffectively) and *Overly Connected* (so afraid of what is happening that they cling to one another and are afraid to function as individuals).

A week or two after the heart attack (point C), family members have begun to modify their responses: they remain *Overly Connected* to each other, afraid to leave each other's sight for fear something else terrible will happen. However, they now have gone from being *Overly Flexible* to the opposite extreme of *Inflexible.* They are clinging to rules, roles, and behavior patterns, grasping at any straw that they hope will bring them back into balance.

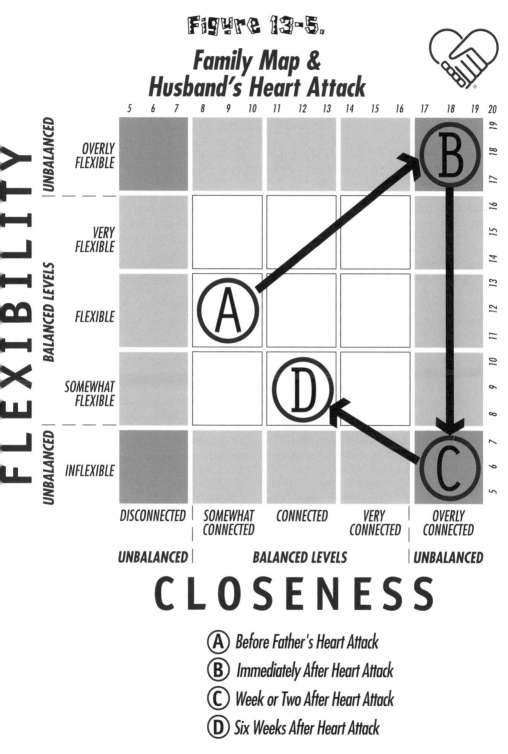

Figure 13-5.

Family Map & Husband's Heart Attack

FLEXIBILITY

UNBALANCED
- OVERLY FLEXIBLE

BALANCED LEVELS
- VERY FLEXIBLE
- FLEXIBLE
- SOMEWHAT FLEXIBLE

UNBALANCED
- INFLEXIBLE

DISCONNECTED | SOMEWHAT CONNECTED | CONNECTED | VERY CONNECTED | OVERLY CONNECTED

UNBALANCED | BALANCED LEVELS | UNBALANCED

CLOSENESS

(A) Before Father's Heart Attack

(B) Immediately After Heart Attack

(C) Week or Two After Heart Attack

(D) Six Weeks After Heart Attack

254

About six weeks after the father's heart attack, the family is progressing steadily toward healthy function again. They have moved into the balanced area of the Family Map (point D) called *Connected* and *Somewhat Flexible*. Their fears have subsided somewhat as the father's condition has stabilized after heart surgery, and so their level of closeness is better balanced. Family members are comfortable being away from each other more often *(Connected)*. In terms of family flexibility, they are now *Somewhat Flexible* in their approach to the inevitable stressors of life; they are neither rigid (stunned and immobilized by the crisis) nor are they buffeted here and there by the winds of change *(Overly Flexible)*. The prognosis is good that the father will survive the heart attack and the family is well on its way to successfully adapting to weather a severe crisis.

"Dad's heart attack was a terrible blow to our family," recalled Angie who was a sophomore in college at the time. "He was only 52 years old when it happened. I used to think 52 was old, but when you think your dad's going to die, 52 doesn't seem very old at all. At first, we didn't have any idea what was going to happen, but we feared for the worst, and we were so confused and upset, we fumbled around and couldn't accomplish anything positive. We wouldn't leave each other's sight for fear somebody else would be struck down. Everyone was in shock and if it weren't for our relatives who came to help us, we would have all fallen apart. They came to the hospital, and stayed with us, and cooked meals, and did a lot of the organizing when we simply couldn't function."

"After about a week the shock seemed to wear off. We still clung together and cried a lot. We knew life had to go on somehow, but we didn't know how to function without Dad there. He had always been the breadwinner and the rock of the family. Now he was down, and we didn't know if he would live. We were locked into our old ways and couldn't figure out new ways to act."

"Fortunately, we figured things out. Dad was going to be out of work for a few months according to the doctors, and we needed some more money coming in. Mom had never worked outside the home since before we kids were born, but she got a job at a friend's office, and Bobbie and I both picked up part-time jobs to help."

"Heat attacks are terrible. There's no doubt about that. But a really good thing happened through all this. We learned how much we loved each other and cared for each other, and we learned that we can live through a hurricane together if we try. Dad has been very proud of us."

Changes in Family Type Over Time

Families change their levels of closeness and flexibility as their circumstances change and as time passes. Even in the early years of marriage, closeness and flexibility can change relatively dramatically. Figure 13-6 shows the changes one young couple go through in a period of only five years. As a serious dating couple (1), Norm and Rachel begin their relationship as *Very Flexible/Connected.* They feel very connected and have a very flexible style in terms of leadership and decision making.

After marriage (2), the *Flexible/Overly Connected* style best describes the newlywed couple's relationship. They are only somewhat flexible because they are still getting organized in terms of their roles and leadership. Being in love and enjoying spending as much time as possible together helps to keep them overly connected.

By the end of their first year of marriage (3), the so-called honeymoon effect wears off and they become *Somewhat Flexible* and *Very Connected.* Their excitement with each other is not as great as it once was (a typical change), their togetherness has dropped into a more balanced range, and their flexibility has decreased somewhat. Their relationship is now a balanced one because both their closeness and their flexibility are at balanced levels.

Another year passes. Baby Evan arrives, and Norm and Rachel are forced to adapt to this new member of their family (4). Life is hectic and the family continues to thrive and is happy being *Overly Flexible/Connected.* The birth of a baby is a momentous time in any couple's relationship. Change is inevitably high. Having a totally dependent and demanding infant changes the lives of this young mother and young father and puts many pressures on their relationship. Their life is in relative turmoil. They are up a couple of times each night to feed the baby and Rachel has quit her job. They can't go out with friends the way they used to, they're short on money, and there are 8 to 12 diapers to change each day. But they are so busy that they don't have time to think about how chaotic their life has become. Evan's presence has increased the couple's sense of bonding and they feel united in their goal of rearing a happy, healthy child.

Eight years have passed since this young couple began to date. Their child is four years old (5). Life has stabilized, and they are functioning as a *Somewhat Flexible* and *Somewhat Connected* family.

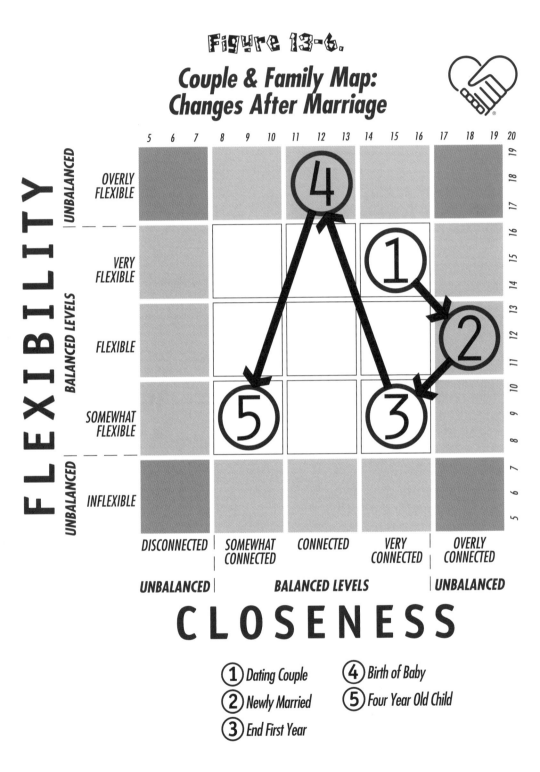

Figure 13-6.
Couple & Family Map: Changes After Marriage

FLEXIBILITY

UNBALANCED

OVERLY FLEXIBLE

BALANCED LEVELS

VERY FLEXIBLE

FLEXIBLE

SOMEWHAT FLEXIBLE

UNBALANCED

INFLEXIBLE

DISCONNECTED | SOMEWHAT CONNECTED | CONNECTED | VERY CONNECTED | OVERLY CONNECTED

UNBALANCED | BALANCED LEVELS | UNBALANCED

CLOSENESS

(1) Dating Couple   (4) Birth of Baby

(2) Newly Married   (5) Four Year Old Child

(3) End First Year

They are experiencing very few changes now. Rachel is home caring for and enjoying Evan. Norm also spends some time with him. They are enjoying the stability (less flexibility), especially in comparison with the chaos they experienced when Evan was born. Their closeness level has dropped off somewhat. Rachel is more involved with the baby than Norm is. Although he is aware of the demands his work places on him, Norm cannot control them to the extent he would like. He is more and more involved in his job and less involved in his family.

In summary, this couple changed over time and experienced various types of family systems. The changes they experienced are rather common and even predictable. The partners' chances for satisfaction increase if their relationship dynamics change as a way of coping with stress. In fact, this couple/family would have had more problems if they had resisted changing their relationship to deal with the new demands.

The three basic qualities of closeness, flexibility, and communication have been identified as qualities that make families strong. The Family Map (the Circumplex Model), a tool for understanding couple and family relationships, is based on these three qualities. It is especially useful for understanding how family relationships change as time passes and life circumstances evolve. The more we know about how relationships work well in families, the better.

〜

Now that you have completed Chapter 13 on Understanding Your Family, go back to the front of the chapter and take the Family Quiz again, this time answer how you would like your family to be (Ideal Family). Then plot your Ideal Family on the Family Map and compare your current vs. ideal.

Postscript:
Looking to Your Future

Hopefully, you have found this book helpful in understanding how to develop and maintain healthy relationships with others. The book is designed so that you can read it again and again so that you are reminded of the important ideas.

We wish you well as you continue to apply what you have learned in this book about building relationships with others. Remember that it takes time and effort to develop and maintain close relationships with others.

Whether you are at school, home or work, the quality of your life and your ultimate success will depend as much by your relationships skills as well as your expertise. By using the relationship skills and ideas taught in this book and course, you will be able to create a happier and more fulfilling life for yourself and others.

In closing, we wish you much success in your personal relationships with others (friends and family) and, eventually in your marriage and family life.